Collection Management for Youth

Responding to the Needs of Learners

SANDRA HUGHES-HASSELL / JACQUELINE C. MANCALL

AMERICAN LIBRARY ASSOCIATION
Chicago   2005

The paper used in this publication meets the minimum requirements of American National Standard for Information Sciences—Permanence of Paper for Printed Library Materials, ANSI Z39.48-1992. ∞

Library of Congress Cataloging-in-Publication Data

Hughes-Hassell, Sandra.
    Collection management for youth : responding to the needs of learners /
Sandra Hughes-Hassell, Jacqueline C. Mancall.
        p.   cm.
    Includes bibliographical references and index.
    ISBN 0-8389-0894-2
    1. School libraries—Collection development. 2. Instructional materials
centers—Collection development. 3. School librarian participation in curriculum
planning. 4. Educational change. 5. Constructivism (Education) I. Mancall,
Jacqueline C., 1932- II. Title.
    Z675.S3H73 2005
    025.2′1878--dc22   2004026911

Printed in the United States of America

09   08   07   06   05   5   4   3   2   1

CONTENTS

part three

Tools for Learner-Centered Collection Management   77

FIGURES

TABLES

ACKNOWLEDGMENTS

The authors of this book would like to thank the many individuals whose work, past and present, has stimulated our thinking and deepened our understanding.

We would also like to thank the Office of Commonwealth Libraries, Bureau of Library Development, Pennsylvania Department of Education for inviting us to create materials and train trainers in new concepts in collection development. This experience was seminal in the development of the concepts of Learner-Centered Collection Development and Collaborative Access Environments.

A special thanks to the school library media specialists in New York City, Philadelphia, and Bucks County, Pennsylvania, who allowed us to share their stories with the readers of this book.

And we thank the editorial staff at the American Library Association, especially Patrick Hogan and Laura Pelehach, for their great patience and helpfulness throughout the long process leading to the final manuscript.

Finally, we thank our families for their support and encouragement.

INTRODUCTION
The Library as a Place for Learning

The concept of the school library media center as a place for learning is not new; however, the application of the concept is undergoing change. In the contemporary environment of information services there is a call for an expanded vision of how both real and virtual materials can be selected to support a learning paradigm that enables the development of information literacy. This vision is strongly articulated in the national guidelines, *Information Power: Building Partnerships for Learning* (American Association of School Librarians and Association for Educational Communications and Technology 1998). The document is intended to set the stage for collaborative school library media services for youth that meet the needs of learners.

We believe that developing and managing a school library media collection that enables learning and supports the development of information literacy raise a number of questions for collection management:

Who is the learner?

What impact does an educational paradigm that focuses on the student as learner have on collection management?

What model can the collection developer use to plan and measure the impact of the collection on the learner?

What roles does the collection manager play in developing a collection that is used to enable learning?

What strategies and tools for planning and accountability can be used to demonstrate the success of a learner-centered collection management process?

We argue that in order to answer these questions, school library media specialists must reimagine their collection management role, becoming *learner-centered collection managers* who act as change agents, leaders, learners, and resource guides (see figure I.1). We envision learner-centered collection managers working collaboratively and building on educational theory and practice to create policy, negotiate budgets, and select resources and access points that enable student learning. To accomplish those tasks, learner-centered collection managers must achieve four goals:

Goal 1: Adopt a learner-centered model of collection management that guides collection decisions and demonstrates accountability in the educational process

Goal 2: Redefine their roles as collection managers in the learner-centered model to support the concept of the library media specialist as teacher and as information guide

Goal 3: Apply appropriate strategies and tools for working in the learner-centered collection paradigm that demonstrates a businesslike perspective based on knowledge of learners, guidance to available resources, and awareness of the uniqueness of the school library media center and community setting

Goal 4: Form a community of practice that shares responsibility for defining, developing, and evaluating the delivery of information resources to support learning

Our purpose in writing this book is to enable school library media specialists to meet each of these goals, thus empowering them to develop and manage collections that enable student learning and support information literacy. The concepts and tools we present were developed with a community perspective in mind. Recognizing that there is a broad range of players who work with the school library media specialist—the principal, teachers, students, parents, public librarians, consortium partners, and appropriate community agencies—our focus is on how the school's broad learning community can most effectively develop and manage collections that meet the changing needs of learners.

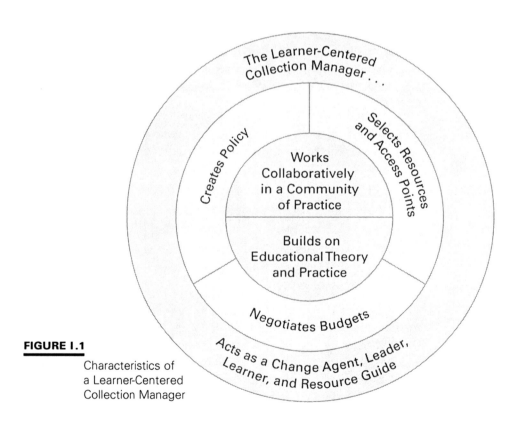

FIGURE I.1

Characteristics of a Learner-Centered Collection Manager

The Approach of This Book

Our approach extends the basic advice on collection development available in current texts that address the process for general as well as specialized clienteles. Such texts set out the issues and criteria for development of policy, selection and removal of materials, budgeting, cooperation among libraries, and the like. The literature on these topics is extensive, and we do not intend to repeat in detail many of the basic and well-tested ideas already offered.[1] Instead, the chapters in our book build on those basics from the perspective of how a collection adapts to the varied and local needs of its learning community.

The ideas, philosophy, and tools we present reflect what we have learned from providing workshops on learner-centered collection development in many areas of the country: for local school districts, library media students, and practitioners attending professional meetings at the local, state, and national levels.[2] We were also influenced by the tools and strategies included in *The Information-Powered School* (Hughes-Hassell and Wheelock 2001)—strategies and tools that were found to be successful in the seven hundred schools involved in the DeWitt Wallace–Reader's Digest Fund National Library Power project. In that book, the author of "Using the Information-Powered School" (Wheelock 2001, 1) asked, "How can we best use our resources so that all students will achieve in school?"

Our focus expands the tools and strategies available in *The Information-Powered School* and the ideas offered in *The Planning Guide for Information Power: Building Partnerships for Learning* (American Association of School Librarians 1999). Our purpose is to suggest what we believe are changing expectations for one specific facet of school librarianship, collection development, with the strategies and tools needed to address only that area. The model and tools we are suggesting for collection managers will enable school library media specialists to put in place, and demonstrate, how the philosophy of *Information Power: Building Partnerships for Learning* can be articulated in the collection development process and how accountability for collection decisions can be confirmed.

Overview of This Book

We have divided the book into three sections. In part 1, we lay out the theoretical foundation for learner-centered collection management. We show how paradigm shifts in educational theory and changes in the environment of information services require school library media specialists to reinterpret their responsibilities for collection development and become change agents, resource guides, leaders, and learners.

In part 2, we provide concrete strategies and tools that school library media specialists can use to develop and manage a Collaborative Access Environment—a collection that reflects the characteristics of the learner, the teaching-learning context of the school, changes in the expanding resource knowledge base, and partnerships with the broader learning community. The first three chapters in part 2 deal with basic elements of collection management—policy, selection, and budgeting—from a learner-centered perspective.

The concluding chapter is specifically oriented to what we have learned about collaboration and collaborative strategies for change in the collection area and how a business perspective can assist the learner-centered collector in articulating the central significance of the collection in student learning.

In part 3, we provide reproducible copies of each of the tools discussed in part 2. We hope you will adopt or adapt the tools to create and manage a school library media collection that enables learning in your community.

NOTES

1. Basic models of the collection development process are explained in Evans (2000) as they relate to many types of libraries. Stein and Brown (2002) and Van Orden and Bishop (2001) discuss collection development procedures as they pertain to school library media service.

2. Our work on learner-centered collection began with a contract from the Office of Commonwealth Libraries, the State Library Agency of Pennsylvania, to create materials and train trainers in new concepts in collection development. The topic had surfaced as one of high concern in a state survey. We collaborated with Debra Kachel to develop materials and trained trainers in Pennsylvania during 2000. From that point, our work on learner-centered collection development was frequently requested, resulting in the delivery of workshops for (1) the Pennsylvania School Librarians Association (PSLA) Annual Conference, (2) the School District of Philadelphia, (3) AASL, (4) two ALA annual meetings, and (5) in New York City for the Robin Hood Foundation in their professional development projects with the New York City public schools.

RECOMMENDED PROFESSIONAL RESOURCES

American Association of School Librarians. 1999. *A Planning Guide for Information Power: Building Partnerships for Learning.* Chicago: American Library Association.

American Association of School Librarians and Association for Educational Communications and Technology. 1998. *Information Power: Building Partnerships for Learning.* Chicago: American Library Association.

Evans, G. Edward. 2000. *Developing Library and Information Center Collections.* 4th ed. Englewood, CO: Libraries Unlimited.

Hughes-Hassell, Sandra, and Anne Wheelock, eds. 2001. *The Information-Powered School.* Chicago: American Library Association.

Stein, Barbara L., and Risa W. Brown. 2002. *Running a School Library Media Center.* 2nd ed. New York: Neal-Schuman.

Van Orden, Phyllis J., and Kay Bishop. 2001. *The Collection Program in Schools.* 3rd ed. Englewood, CO: Libraries Unlimited.

Wheelock, Anne. 2001. "Using the Information-Powered School." In *The Information-Powered School,* ed. Sandra Hughes-Hassell and Anne Wheelock, 1–3. Chicago: American Library Association.

part one

The Theoretical Foundation for Learner-Centered Collection Management

1

Changing Expectations and Models for Practice

A number of factors influence how we build and manage what we have traditionally referred to as *the collection*. Paramount among them is the proliferating body and nature of information that is available. As important is the paradigm shift in learning theory that is changing the teaching-learning context of the school. As we show in this chapter, both factors have major implications for practice for the collector and for the manager of the school library media center as a resource place.[1]

CHANGE 1
The Paradigm Shift in Education

During the last decade, our view of teaching and learning has undergone a change. At all levels of education, kindergarten to college, there is a growing awareness of what it means to enable learning. The model in which students are passive receptors of knowledge has not been universally successful. Making teachers better speakers and lecturers has not produced better learners. The paradigm has shifted from an emphasis on good teaching to an emphasis on enabling learning. This has major implications for school library media programs and library collections, and for the collector.

Traditional theories of learning, which have influenced teaching and learning for more than a century, view education and learning as external processes. Students learn a prescribed body of knowledge through memorization and drill, with knowledge viewed as true and unchanging. Strategies for learning focus on the teacher as the source of knowledge and students as recipients. The aim is to provide students with a common core of concepts, skills, and knowledge (Walker and Lambert 1995; Brooks and Brooks 1993; Barr and Tagg 1995).

In traditional classrooms, the focus is on developing the conventional academic intelligences (Gardner 1983). As table 1.1 shows, direct instruction is the primary teaching strategy. Teachers establish learning goals, determine the criteria for success, deliver the content in "bits" and "chunks," and evaluate student progress using standardized tests. Curricular activities rely heavily on textbooks (Walker and Lambert 1995; Brooks and Brooks 1993; Barr and Tagg 1995).

TABLE 1.1

The Traditional View of Learning

Traditional Theory of Learning	*Traditional Learning Context*
Learning is viewed as an external process.	Students are viewed as "empty vessels" that are filled by the teacher.
Knowledge is viewed as true and unchanging.	Focus is on providing students with a common core of concepts, knowledge, and skills.
Knowledge comes in "chunks" and "bits" and is delivered by teachers.	Direct instruction is the primary teaching strategy; textbooks provide the bulk of content.
Outcomes of learning are uniform.	Teachers determine the outcomes and learning is measured by standardized tests.

As we progressed through the twentieth century, a new theory of learning emerged. This theory, known as constructivism, views education as "an internal process in which learners use prior knowledge and experience to share meaning and construct knowledge" (Walker and Lambert 1995, 20). Central to constructivism is the belief that knowledge is not a static body of information but rather a process. The role of the teacher is to bring preexisting knowledge to the surface, provide learners with experiences that challenge their current understandings, and make learners aware of the processes they use to create new structures (Walker and Lambert 1995; Brooks and Brooks 1993; Barr and Tagg 1995). The aim of constructivism is "education for understanding" (Gardner 1983).

As table 1.2 shows, constructivist classrooms look different. Constructivism advances the idea that learning is a social endeavor requiring engagement with others. Students work in groups to solve problems together. Inquiry and Socratic dialogue are the key teaching strategies. Curricular activities rely heavily on primary sources, experiments, and manipulatives. Students and teachers establish learning goals together and assessment involves self-reflection and demonstrations. In this environment, the challenge of collection development is the selection of resources and access points that support the interests, talents, and abilities of *all* learners.

TABLE 1.2

The Constructivist View of Learning

Constructivist Theory of Learning	*Constructivist Learning Context*
Learning is viewed as a process. Knowledge is viewed as constantly changing; knowledge and beliefs are formed within the learner. Learning is a social activity that is enhanced by shared inquiry. Knowledge is constructed by the learner through interactions with ideas, objects, and people. The values and beliefs of learners affect how they interpret and assign meaning to their experiences. Outcomes are varied and often unpredictable.	Students are treated as thinkers with emerging theories about the world. Students are involved in authentic learning tasks; use of multiple intelligences is stressed. Students are engaged in cooperative learning. Inquiry and Socratic dialogue are key teaching strategies; primary resources and manipulatives are used. Students are encouraged to make connections to prior learning and personal experience; opportunities are provided for students to reflect on their own learning. Students and teachers together determine outcomes; assessment involves students in self-reflection and demonstrations.

CHANGE 2
The Proliferating Body and Nature of Information

The information world continues to change at a rapid pace. Vendors have moved quickly to create new products and new markets. A plethora of online searching environments are now available commercially that allow user-oriented searching across multiple databases. The best-known reference format, the encyclopedia, is available in multiple formats, including those with photos, videos, animation, documentaries, maps, tables, and sound clips. Advanced networking and online connections, cable and satellite hookups, and other technological devices provide access to information resources around the globe.

Keeping up with new resources, advances in online searching, and changes in technology and delivery mechanisms is a challenge for school library media specialists. In order to develop and manage collections that enable learning, media specialists must grapple with such questions as

How does the collector remain current about new resources, emerging formats, and information delivery mechanisms?

What impact do emerging formats have on the unique users of the collection?

What changes need to be made to resource and access policies to reflect changes in the information environment?

What changes need to be made to the budgeting process to provide access to information in a variety of formats?

What role do consortia play in providing resources for youth?

How does the collector develop mechanisms to alert and connect constituents to resources?

CHANGE 3
Evolving Models of Collection Management

Three gradually evolving models of collection management show the intellectual stages we have followed in moving our view of collection management to a constructivist approach. The first, the Collection-Centered Model, is the one most often described in the literature and the one best understood by experienced school library media specialists. The second, the Learner-Centered Model, projects the concepts we believe must be considered in making collection management decisions for learners. The third and final model, the Collaborative Access Environment, broadly pictures the collection management world as a setting for learning.

The Collection-Centered Model

The most traditional approach to collection management is the Collection-Centered Model (CCM). It places the school library media specialist in the position of resource expert, a difficult position to maintain in today's rapidly changing information environment. Quality is usually the overriding concern, with determination of quality coming from independent outside sources. The focus is on development of a set of materials that meet quality criteria established in policy. Various informational formats are considered, with a focus on buying what is the best "just in case" it may be requested. Suggestions from the learning community have a place in this traditional process, although they are vetted by the school library media specialist, who is seen as the expert and is the person who controls the purse for the collection's materials. It should be noted that in the traditional school setting the curriculum is the guiding factor in determining the subject areas collected. Curriculum continues to be the central concern but is reconsidered as we move toward other models.

The traditional collection-development model supports a teaching-centered paradigm, with library materials purchased just in case they are needed. Figure 1.1 suggests a picture for this process. As the model shows, developing a quality collection is the central focus of the collection-centered approach. Policy directs what is allowed to be selected. Selection is guided by reviewers considered experts and by the reviewing media. Acquisition of materials is often based on the broad services jobbers and vendors can offer. Weeding or removal of materials tends to entail the examination of every item within the collection, and is usually a time-consuming and often neglected part of collection control. Use of the CCM suggests that the collector is in the position of supporting traditional expectations. The collection per se is the central consideration.

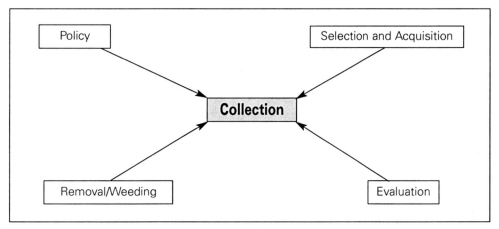

FIGURE 1.1

The Collection-Centered Model (CCM)

The Learner-Centered Model

While the CCM is adequate for a teacher-centered learning environment where direct instruction is the primary teaching strategy, if we accept the teaching and learning principles outlined in table 1.2, then we have to consider the implications for the collector and contemplate a revised approach. The Learner-Centered Model (LCM) of collection development, shown in figure 1.2, sets the stage for the approach and tools we have developed.

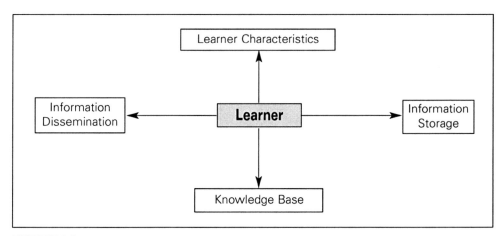

FIGURE 1.2

The Learner-Centered Model (LCM)

Note the central label, *Learner,* in this model. In order to build success for the learner, data are needed to describe

The *learner characteristics* of those using the library media setting and its physical and virtual collection

The *knowledge base* for the currency and level of information the learner must acquire to meet his or her needs at various times

Information storage decisions that include what can be stored, that is, classified and described using traditional cataloging and classification tools

Information dissemination, or the various strategies for bringing knowledge at the learner's level to the individual, including materials accessible through conventional circulation procedures as well as through virtual access to databases, electronic serial subscriptions, and so forth

Throughout the Learner-Centered Model our collector becomes a *guide* rather than an expert. Our guide provides access to the virtual world of information and to knowledgeable individuals who can offer subject and learner specific advice, expanding the potential utility of materials and information the learner encounters.

The Collaborative Access Environment

The third and final model, shown in figure 1.3, may be the most significant one in a world where tools for access beyond the local school are becoming more widely used at the same time that financial resources are becoming more limited. We term this model a Collaborative Access Environment (CAE) and introduce it in this chapter and reinforce it in those that follow.

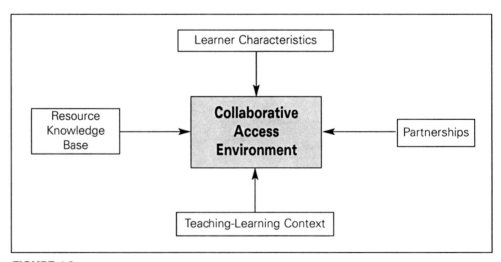

FIGURE 1.3

The Collaborative Access Environment (CAE)

The CAE is influenced by constantly shifting patterns in its internal and external relationships. There is no beginning point and no set of linear steps for the collector who operates within this configuration. Instead, the Collaborative Access Environment is controlled by systematic reactions to multiple changing forces. In our diagram the forces are learner characteristics, teaching and learning context, resource knowledge base, and partnerships. Each of those forces requires data to support decision making and policy to clarify relationships and expectations. The successful collector in this model is a *guide* who understands the needs, interests, and capabilities of the school and its learners. The focus is both on collecting and on making available the most appropriate materials just in time.

LEARNER CHARACTERISTICS

The learners in our model include all the members of the school community: the students, the teachers, the administrators, the parents, and the caregivers. Available socioeconomic data describe the broad characteristics of those individuals and provide one frame of reference that will influence resource and access decisions. Data on specific student abilities come from information collected by the school, such as reading levels, and from interactions with students, teachers, parents, and caregivers.

TEACHING AND LEARNING CONTEXT

Data needed to understand the teaching-learning context come from close observation in classrooms, planning meetings with the teaching staff, professional development opportunities, and analysis of units that require resource support. Mechanisms exist for curriculum analysis and may be useful first steps in looking at the broad picture and making a first stab at matching materials to the teaching and learning context.

RESOURCE KNOWLEDGE BASE

The resource knowledge base is in a state of continuous change. This is particularly evident in areas like science, technology, and medicine but can also be seen in areas like the social sciences, psychology, and fine arts. The growth of the knowledge base has been accelerated by changes in technology. The Internet has made instant access to people, ideas, documents, images, and sounds possible. Members of the learning community can now interact with each other across cultural, social, and distance barriers. This means that they can share information freely and work together to create new understandings.

PARTNERSHIPS

In a Collaborative Access Environment, teams and partnerships become the key elements in collection management. The school library media specialist collaborates with teachers, the public library, and other community-based organizations to provide access to a wide variety of resources that enable learning.

Conclusion

Paradigm shifts in education, changes in the information environment, and evolving models of collection development require school library media specialists to rethink the collection development process. As we will show in part 2 of this book, when redesigning the collection to make it learner-centered, school library media specialists must keep in mind that

> Changes in learner-characteristics and the teaching-learning context need to be taken into consideration in developing policy and selecting materials and access points
>
> The content of material must support the mission, goals, and strategies of the educational organization serving youth
>
> Selection and budgeting must be connected to assessment and accountability
>
> Legal and ethical issues, such as intellectual freedom, copyright, Internet access, and information ethics, must continue to be part of collection and access decisions
>
> Collaboration and partnerships with the broader community are critical to providing resources that meet the requirements of the learning community

NOTE

1. We first discussed the concepts, theories, and models identified in this chapter in Sandra M. Hughes and Jacqueline C. Mancall, "Developing a Collaborative Access Environment: Meeting the Resource Needs of the Learning Community," in *Student Learning in an Information Age: Principles and Practice,* ed. Barbara K. Stripling, (Englewood, CO: Libraries Unlimited, 1999), 231–259.

RECOMMENDED PROFESSIONAL RESOURCES

Barr, Robert B., and John Tagg. 1995. "From Teaching to Learning—A New Paradigm for Undergraduate Education." *Change* (Nov./Dec.): 13–25.

Brooks, Jacqueline G., and Martin G. Brooks. 1993. *In Search of Understanding: The Case for Constructivist Classrooms.* Alexandria, VA: Association for Supervision and Curriculum Development.

Gardner, Howard. 1983. *Frames of Mind.* New York: Basic Books.

Hughes, Sandra M., and Jacqueline C. Mancall. 1999. "Developing a Collaborative Access Environment: Meeting the Resource Needs of the Learning Community." In *Student Learning in an Information Age: Principles and Practice,* ed. Barbara K. Stripling, 231–259. Englewood, CO: Libraries Unlimited.

Stripling, Barbara K. 2003. "Inquiry-Based Learning." In *Curriculum Connections through the Library,* ed. B. K. Stripling and S. Hughes-Hassell, 3–40. Englewood, CO: Libraries Unlimited.

Walker, Deborah, and Linda Lambert. 1995. "Learning and Leading Theory: A Century in the Making." In *The Constructivist Leader,* ed. Linda Lambert et al., 1–27. New York: Teachers College Press.

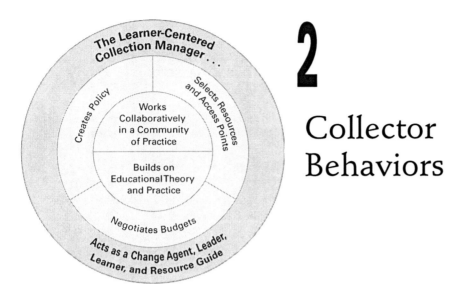

The Learner-Centered Collection Manager...

Creates Policy

Selects Resources and Access Points

Works Collaboratively in a Community of Practice

Builds on Educational Theory and Practice

Negotiates Budgets

Acts as a Change Agent, Leader, Learner, and Resource Guide

2

Collector Behaviors

As the context in which school library media specialists work continues to change, assumptions about the role of the collector must also change. In order to provide resources that meet the requirements of the learning community, not only must school library media specialists reimagine the collection and create access environments that reflect the characteristics of the learner, the teaching-learning context of the school, changes in the resource knowledge base, and partnerships with the broader learning community, but they must also reinterpret their role in collection development. As table 2.1 shows, learner-centered collection managers act as resource guides, change agents, leaders, and learners.

Resource Guide

In chapter 1, we identified the role of the collector as guide rather than expert. We believe the role of guide is appropriate for three reasons. First, in today's ever-changing information world the school library media specialist can no longer be the sole proprietor of a self-contained, one-stop-shopping establishment. Even extending the metaphor to operating an information supermarket is inappropriate. School library media specialists must learn how to manage kiosks on the information superhighway, kiosks that are staffed by a variety of experts, carry a minimal and ever-changing stock, and provide instant access to other stores of items and to resource people wherever they are located.

Second, changes in educational theory and practice in the last decade necessitate that teachers be knowledgeable about resources. For example, the balanced literacy approach to reading instruction requires elementary-school teachers to be acquainted with books developed by publishers to support early

TABLE 2.1

Collector Behaviors in Learner-Centered Collection Management

REQUIRED COLLECTOR BEHAVIORS
Resource Guide   Collaborates with teaching and learning teams, students, parents, and other members of the learning community to select resources that enable desired learner outcomes   Develops a process for gaining input on collection decisions from all members of the learning community   Provides continual assessment of emerging resources and delivery mechanisms   Evaluates, on a continual basis, the match between available resources, learner characteristics, and the teaching and learning context   Develops mechanisms to alert and connect constituents to resources   Facilitates physical and intellectual access to all resources in all formats   *Change Agent*   Brings members of the learning community into the collection and access decision-making process   Promotes a collaborative culture in the school   Supports the learning community in the use of resources to enable learning   Models the use of resources to address local, state, and national standards   *Leader*   Revises and updates resource and access policies and practices to reflect both a learner-centered paradigm of teaching and learning, and changes in the information environment   Creates and manages internal and external cooperative arrangements to meet the needs of the learning community   Develops a budget that maximizes access to resources   *Learner*   Understands the implications of learning theory on collection and access decisions   Remains current about new resources and emerging formats and information-delivery mechanisms

literacy development. In social studies and history classes, the use of primary documents has become common, thus requiring teachers to be familiar with resources like the Library of Congress American Memory Collection. Teachers bring expertise to the selection process—expertise that the school library media specialist acting as a guide recognizes and taps into.

Third, in learner-centered classrooms, library resources are no longer viewed as supplemental. Instead, they are considered central to the success of the learner. Alerting the learning community to new resources, as well as to emerging developments in technology, is a critical guiding role for the school library media specialist.

Change Agent

The Collaborative Access Environment (CAE) requires school library media specialists, teachers, and other members of the learning community to enter into collaborative relationships and share authority for collection development and access decisions—neither of which is a familiar experience for most educators. Generally, teachers work in isolation in their own classrooms and they expect school library media specialists to take sole responsibility for choosing library resources. In order to be successful learner-centered collectors, then, school library media specialists must become change agents—modifying the perceptions of teachers and encouraging them to become active partners in the collection process.

At the same time, providing access to information is not enough. School library media specialists must also share their expertise in using resources with teachers and other members of the learning community. They must model the use of resources to address standards of learning and to solve instructional problems and support teachers as they attempt to incorporate electronic databases, primary documents, multimedia resources, and other sources of information into their teaching.

Leader

Information Power: Building Partnerships for Learning (American Association of School Librarians and Association for Educational Communications and Technology 1998) identifies leadership as a key role for school library media specialists. For the collector, leadership means encouraging collaboration skills in other members of the learning community, thinking about the future and anticipating emerging technologies, partnering with libraries and other agencies within the community to share resources and to engage in cooperative negotiations for better pricing, and revising and updating resource and access policies.

Leadership also means planning and managing a budget that maximizes access to resources. Many school library media specialists are accustomed to being given a lump-sum or line-item budget based on a per-student allocation—an allocation determined by central office or school board personnel. This type of budgeting is inadequate for collection management that is responsive to the needs of the learning community. Instead, school library media specialists must become adept at developing and presenting budgets on an annual basis to the school council, site-based team, and even the board of education.

Learner

As Jose-Marie Griffiths points out, we cannot always lead. Sometimes we need to "follow while someone else steps up for a while and cuts down the forest in front of us, clearing a new path" (1998, 8). Our success as learner-centered collectors depends on our ability to continue to be learners.

As long as educators, politicians, and the general public continue to debate the purposes, processes, and structures of education, educational practice will continue to change. School library media specialists must stay abreast of how educational research, policy, and legislation are affecting the teaching-learning context, including standards for student learning, teaching strategies and assessments, and state and national accountability measures. At the building level, school library media specialists must understand how such changes are being interpreted and what impact they have on collection and access decisions.

Changes in the information world also show no indication of slowing down. Keeping up with new resources, advances in online searching, and changes in technology and delivery mechanisms is a necessity for collectors who are striving to match resources to the needs of the learner.

Conclusion

So far in this book we have discussed the theoretical foundation for learner-centered collection management and explained the changes needed in the attitudes and behaviors of school library media specialists working in a Collaborative Access Environment.

In figure 2.1 we present a framework for implementing a Learner-Centered Model and developing a Collaborative Access Environment. As the framework indicates, the process is dynamic and ongoing. Each piece of the framework remains open to change in order to respond to the variable needs of the learning community.

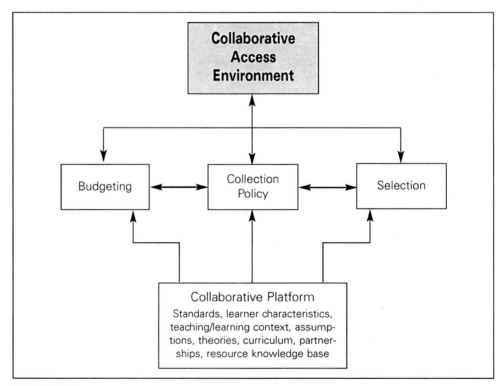

FIGURE 2.1

Framework for Implementing a Learner-Centered Model

The collaborative platform reflects standards of practice, learner characteristics, the teaching-learning context of the school, the curriculum that is in place, and partnerships that have been developed for resource access. This platform is constantly interacting with all pieces of the collaborative collection development environment.

The collection policy is developed by working with identified stakeholders in the school community.

The selection process takes into consideration the characteristics of the learners and ongoing assessment of the collection in terms of its ability to deliver appropriate materials and resources that support student learning.

Budgeting reflects the priorities of the school community for delivering the curriculum and supporting the students' personal information needs.

In part 2 we will expand on the elements of the framework and present strategies and tools we believe will enable school library media specialists to make CAE a reality in their schools.

RECOMMENDED PROFESSIONAL RESOURCES

American Association of School Librarians and Association for Educational Communications and Technology. 1998. *Information Power: Building Partnerships for Learning.* Chicago: American Library Association.

Griffiths, Jose-Marie. 1998. "The New Information Professional." *Bulletin of the American Society for Information Science* 24 (Feb./Mar.): 8–12.

Lambert, Linda. 2003. *Leadership Capacity for Lasting School Improvement.* Alexandria, VA: Association for Supervision and Curriculum Development.

Walker, Deborah, and Linda Lambert. 1995. "Learning and Leading Theory: A Century in the Making." In *The Constructivist Leader,* ed. Linda Lambert et al., 1–27. New York: Teachers College Press.

part two

Strategies for Learner-Centered Collection Management

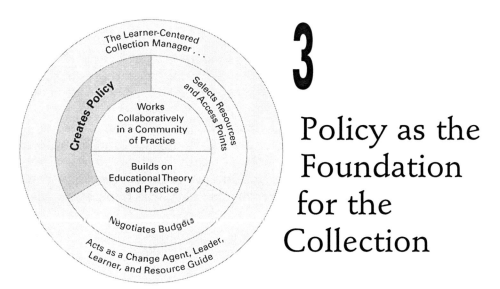

The Learner-Centered
Collection Manager...

Selects Resources
and Access Points

Creates Policy

Works
Collaboratively
in a Community
of Practice

Builds on
Educational Theory
and Practice

Negotiates Budgets

Acts as a Change Agent, Leader,
Learner, and Resource Guide

3
Policy as the Foundation for the Collection

Policy is the guiding element in a local move toward a learner-centered collection. It provides guidance to the library media center staff, directs collection actions at all levels, and, as important, informs the clientele what to expect from the library media center collection and resource access services. Developing a learner-centered collection requires a plan, one in which the community to be served is involved in making decisions and is described in sufficient detail to clarify what, where, and how a broad range of resources will be made available to them. *Policy* becomes the written plan. Clear, written policy creates stability and continuity in collection activities and indicates that the library media center is a businesslike operation willing to be accountable for its actions. Policy is impersonal and safeguards the clientele from individual collector biases. It provides the basis for development of procedures that increase efficiency in all collection operations, including a format for how financial resources are to be allocated and complaints are to be handled.[1]

Since policy is the result of planning, it is essential for the school library media specialist to understand and apply an open planning process as policy is developed, tested, and approved. Advice and a number of planning models exist in the library literature. Some of the more current ones are suggested at the end of this chapter. Below we consider the basic elements of policy and the nine steps for bringing the stakeholders in your learning community into the application of those elements as you develop learner-centered collection policy.

Basic Elements of Policy

Many authors have documented the sections that are found in written policy and that should be included.[2] Basic elements that have been identified in existing collection policies are described in table 3.1.

Learner-Centered Elements of Policy

In a learner-centered policy, the broad labels of written policy elements may remain the same as in a more traditional policy. The change is the incorporation, where applicable, of the concepts and language of Learner-Centered Collection Development. Table 3.2 indicates the direction we are suggesting.

As you compare tables 3.1 and 3.2, you will note that the text in table 3.2 is more specific in calling attention to how collection policy supports the needs of local learners and local curriculum. Although responsibility for selection stays with the library media specialist, the specialist's role shifts from expert to guide so that responsibility for selection of resources is shared with teachers and other

TABLE 3.1

Basic Elements of Collection Policy

Element	*Description*
Introduction	Why a center for materials and resource access should exist
Broad goals	What the collection and its services should achieve
Selection	Criteria for making resource decisions
Responsibility for selection	Library media specialist as expert
Formats	Allowable formats, including electronic
Collection methods	Library budgeted funds, donations and gifts, cooperative agreements
Problem areas	Subject areas with special concerns
Intellectual freedom	Broad access to ideas and prevention of censorship; ALA policy documents and complaint form usually attached
Collection maintenance (weeding)	Criteria for removal of materials that are obsolete or predicted to be of little use
Evaluation	Methods for determining the collection's success in meeting user needs
Confidentiality	Protecting identification of users of specific items
Copyright	What can and cannot be copied for both use and inclusion in the collection
Subject analysis	Description by Dewey (or LC) classification showing the numerical depth of each subject's holding, formats allowable within subject categories, age of materials in a category, and current collecting intensity for a category; in matrix or narrative format within or attached to policy
Electronic information resources	Access to be determined by user demand, relevance, availability, cost, training available, equipment needed, and technical support
Consortia, cooperative agreements, networking	Role of consortia, cooperative agreements, and networking in providing extended access to information
Revision of policy	Who will be responsible for policy change, plus when and how

TABLE 3.2

Basic Elements of Learner-Centered Collection Policy

Element	Learner-Centered Description
Introduction (philosophy and mission)	The collection of materials and access services exist to support the learning needs of the community as described in the collection policy and its appendixes
Broad goals	Materials collected and accessed meet the identified characteristics of the learning community and support the teaching-learning context
Selection	Resource decisions are based on analysis of local learners and curriculum
Responsibility for selection	Library media specialist, acting as guide, works with teachers and other members of the learning community
Formats	Allowable formats based on knowledge of learning styles and preferences, curricular objectives, teaching strategies, and assessment methods
Collection methods	Funds allocated based on zero-based or program budget considerations; donations and gifts must meet policy parameters; cooperative agreements extend access potential
Problem areas	Sensitivity to the racial, ethnic, socioeconomic, and gender composition of the learning community
Intellectual freedom	Broad access to ideas and prevention of censorship; ALA policy documents usually attached
Collection maintenance (weeding)	Criteria for removal of materials that are obsolete or predicted to be of little use; suggested methodologies include collection sampling for usage patterns and the match between resources and learner characteristics
Evaluation	Methods for determining the collection's success in meeting user needs, including how useful and appropriate the collection was in supporting curricular goals and objectives and meeting the learning needs of students
Confidentiality	Protecting identification of users of specific items
Copyright	What can and cannot be copied for both use and inclusion in the collection
Subject analysis	Description by Dewey (or LC) classification showing the numerical depth of each subject's holding, formats allowable within subject categories, age of materials in a category, and current collecting intensity for a category; in matrix or narrative format within or attached to policy; particular attention to categories that have direct curricular relationship
Electronic information resources	Access to be determined by user demand, relevance, availability, cost, training available, equipment needed, and technical support
Consortia, cooperative agreements, networking	Role of consortia, cooperative agreements, and networking in providing extended access to information
Revision of policy	Who will be responsible for policy change, plus when and how; emphasis is on collaboration and involving the learning community in the process

members of the learning community. Allowable material formats are based on knowledge of learning styles, curricular objectives, and preferred teaching and assessment methods. Policy collection methodologies call specific attention to the allocation of collection funds to designated programs. Problem areas and considerations regarding intellectual freedom remain similar in both traditional and learner-centered collection policies.

In the learner-centered policy, collection maintenance is expanded to highlight methods for matching resource usage patterns and learner characteristics when selecting materials for removal. Evaluation techniques are broadened to include how the collection meets the curricular goals of the school and the needs of learners. Confidentiality and copyright concerns remain the same in both approaches to policy, while the learner-centered policy expands subject analysis to pay particular attention to how subject strengths directly relate to curricular areas. Electronic information resources, consortia, cooperative agreements, and networking are also similar under both approaches. However, in learner-centered collection policy, the final element, revision of policy, is expanded into a collaborative effort in which the learning community plays an increasingly important role in maintaining the learner-centered process.

The Collaborative Planning Process

Planning involves identifying what you intend to do in order to grapple systematically with opportunities, problems, and alternative courses of action. Our concern in this chapter is with how understanding of the learning community affects policy elements. Table 3.3 identifies a nine-step process that will bring the stakeholders in your community into the development and approval of your learner-

TABLE 3.3

Steps in Learner-Centered Policy Formation and Revision

Steps	*Responsible Persons*
Step 1: Identify stakeholders	School library media specialist
Step 2: Perform community analysis	School library media specialist
Step 3: Arrange focus group with stakeholders	School library media specialist
Step 4: Set strategic vision and goals	School library media specialist and stakeholder group
Step 5: Prepare first draft of policy	Writing team
Step 6: Test draft of policy	Stakeholder group
Step 7: Revise policy	Writing team
Step 8: Gain approval of policy	School library media specialist and principal
Step 9: Communicate and celebrate	School library media specialist, stakeholder group, and learning community

centered collection policy. Our ideas are influenced, in part, by the advice and planning models that exist in the library literature and the widespread use of SWOT analysis techniques—techniques that call attention to an organization's strengths, weaknesses, opportunities, and threats as strategic planning progresses.[3]

Remember: working on policy is an iterative process. We are suggesting a series of logical steps, but we assume that where local iterations are necessary, they will be added. It is good practice to keep testing the efficacy of policy ideas and to avoid becoming too attached to specific ideas.

STEP 1
Identify Stakeholders

The first step in the planning process is to identify the key stakeholders who should participate in policy development. As we discussed in chapters 1 and 2, the learner-centered collection environment is a collaborative one, and the learning community must be involved in responding to ideas and documents as they are developed. Tool 1, Stakeholder Contact/SWOT Analysis, provides a matrix for performing an initial stakeholder analysis and is intended to be completed by the school library media specialist. (Reproducible copies of all tools can be found in part 3.)

In figure 3.1 we show a completed version of Tool 1 to illustrate the types of individuals that should be part of the planning process, the strengths and weaknesses they bring to the process, and the potential opportunities and threats their presence offers. Such information will be extremely useful as you develop the questions that will guide the discussion when you pull the influential stakeholders together in a meeting. Your local situation will dictate how the blank tool is completed. As you complete the matrix, keep in mind the importance of including at least one representative from each segment of the learning community, and from the student segment in particular.

STEP 2
Perform Community Analysis

Step 2 has a twofold purpose: (1) to determine the kinds of information you need to create a broad focus for describing your learning community and (2) to gather and analyze those data. Such information will be essential as you continue to work with your identified stakeholders in developing policy.

The major tasks of step 2 include:

1. *Identifying community information resources.* Use the forms suggested in Tool 2, Identifying Resources in Your Community, and Tool 3, Identifying Learner Characteristics, to identify the information you need to describe your broad learning community and its resources. Tool 2 helps you to identify useful organizations, institutions, and individuals; the resources each can provide; and who to contact for information. Tool 3 aids you in creating learner descriptions by identifying needed data, the sources of the data, and persons who can give you access to the data. Completed

Stakeholder	Name/Contact Information	Strengths Brought to Process	Weaknesses Brought to Process	Opportunities Brought to Process	Threats Brought to Process
District-level curriculum coordinator		Knowledge of district curriculum emphases and standards for students	Library may not be a high priority in allocation of funds to deliver local standards	Information presented may educate and persuade this critical decision maker to support resource allocations	May suggest inappropriate role for library and its collections. Has influence to restrict financial resources
District-level library coordinator		Knowledge of library holdings in relation to district curriculum emphases and standards for students	Superficial knowledge of individual library's holdings and patterns of use	May act as an advocate based on broad knowledge of resource issues beyond local school	May take a low-profile role. May be intimidated by more powerful stakeholders
School library media specialist		Knowledge of school's true curriculum and characteristics of the learning community	Focus may remain on traditional collection concerns rather than on the changing resource needs of students	Opportunity to influence decision makers. Opportunity to broaden own ideas of what is desirable	Ideas may be challenged and defeated by more powerful stakeholders
Principal		Knowledge of school's areas of emphasis	Library may not be a high priority	Information provided may enhance his or her concept of what the collection and collection services can deliver within the local school	May suggest inappropriate role for library and its collections. Has influence to restrict financial resources
Teacher department/grade representative(s)		Knowledge of units taught, required student outputs/products, and standards to be achieved	May have flawed mental model of types of resources to support subject access	Brings concrete ideas about how units should be supported with resources	May seek to divert resource funds to enhance classroom collections
Public library representative		Knowledge of broad community	Inadequate knowledge of students' learning characteristics and schools' collection	Extends professional knowledge of what is available and how to make holdings compatible across collections. Ability to identify and close subject gaps	Could persuade influential stakeholders that the public library is better able than the school library to support curriculum resources
Consortium representative		Knowledge of consortium characteristics and broad holding patterns of members	Inadequate knowledge of learners' needs within a specific local school	Able to provide sense of subject holding patterns across participating libraries. Can help to develop policy to identify where consortium holdings fit with schools' areas of emphasis	Demands for consortium membership may be antagonistic to ideas of stakeholder

FIGURE 3.1

Completed Version of Tool 1, Stakeholder Contact/SWOT Analysis

FIGURE 3.1

Completed Version of Tool 1, Stakeholder Contact/SWOT Analysis (cont.)

Stakeholder	Name/Contact Information	Strengths Brought to Process	Weaknesses Brought to Process	Opportunities Brought to Process	Threats Brought to Process
Community representative		Knowledge of community resources	Bias toward own interests	Learns about and can influence professional policy that controls library holdings	Could decide resource allocations are not needed due to inappropriate understanding of what the Internet provides
Parent(s)		Knowledge of learner characteristics and community resources	Bias toward own interests	Expands knowledge of collection and collection services May be potential source of funding support	May push own biases for topical coverage
Student(s)		Knowledge of students' perspectives Knowledge of resources (particularly Web resources)	Bias toward own interests	Brings student perspective to selection of resources	May push own biases for topical coverage

versions of Tool 2 and Tool 3 are presented in figure 3.2 and figure 3.3 as examples of what you can learn from a community analysis.[4] The information will vary depending upon your local community and the input from your community members.

2. *Gathering the available data.* Use the data sources identified in Tool 3 to develop a profile of your learners. Make sure to include general information, such as the number and types of students to be served, as well as more specific information, such as students' developmental and intellectual levels, mobility rates, socioeconomic levels, and access to technology at home. Use short e-mail surveys to enrich the data and to learn about your users' (and nonusers') most recent experiences with library materials.

3. *Analyzing the data to produce summaries of your community analysis.* Pick out key results and present them as simply as possible.

The information you gather in step 2 will support your work with the stakeholders you identified in step 1 and will allow you to clarify the basic elements of collection policy as they relate to your specific situation. Information about your learners and the resources available in your community affects all the basic elements of learner-centered policy as it is developed: the introduction, which identifies how the library media center will support the specific community; broad goals, which reflect how the characteristics of the community determine the collection and access goals; specifics on selection of resources, which take into consideration the characteristics of learners; how budgeted funds will be allocated to support programs; and so on.

Organization, Institution, or Individual	Possible Resources	Contact Person
Kensington Branch of The Free Library	ILL, bibliographies, Spanish resources, speakers, access to electronic resources, advice on selection	Children's librarian/ branch head
Multicultural Resource Center	Reviews, bibliographies, resources, advice on selection, speakers	Director
St. Christopher's Children's Hospital	Speakers, field trips	Community liaison
Taller Puertorriqueno Julia de Burgos Book and Craft Store	Spanish resources, advice on selection, speakers (authors and illustrators)	Owner
Keepers of the Culture	Storytellers, resources by and about African and African American culture	President
Asociación de Músicos Latino Americanos	Artists in residence, performances	President
Temple University	ILL, speakers, electronic resources	Community liaison
Wagner Free Institute of Science	Science resources, speakers, field trips	Community liaison
Charles L. Blockson Afro-American Collection	Resources on underground railroad	Community liaison
Kule Mele African-American Dance Ensemble	Artists in residence, African American music	Director

FIGURE 3.2

Completed Version of Tool 2, Identifying Resources in Your Community

Information/Data	Information/Data Source	Contact Person/ Organization
Size of student body	Tenth-day enrollment figures	School secretary
Math, reading, and writing abilities	Report cards, test scores	Principal, assistant principal, teachers
Ethnicity and immigration status	School/home survey, school profile	Pupils, ESL teacher
Curriculum themes (specific to class/grade)	Teachers, grade conferences, standards	District and school
Technological abilities of students	Survey of community	Computer teacher
Special learning needs	School-based support teams, guidance counselors, parents, teachers, observation	Special education teacher
Extracurricular activities	After-school program, special-interest groups	Teachers, parents, pupils, community center
Student mobility (including bus population)	Demographics (Comprehensive Educational Plan [CEP])	Pupils' report cards
Socioeconomic level of community	School CEP, school's report card	Guidance counselor, social workers
Access to home computers/Internet	Informal survey during library orientation	School library media specialist

FIGURE 3.3

Completed Version of Tool 3, Identifying Learner Characteristics

STEP 3
Arrange Focus Group with Stakeholders

Once you have completed the community analysis, it is time to get input from the stakeholders you identified in step 1. We suggest you can achieve your purpose by using a focus group. Your first task is to persuade your stakeholders to work with you on collection policy. Prepare a one-page letter (or e-mail) stating your intent to hold a focus group to share your ideas about the development (or revision) of the library's collection policy. Mention the type of information you are gathering that you believe will influence policy development. Suggest strongly that the ideas of influential members of the learning community are essential. Let your stakeholders know that you will be sending a small set of information items in advance to prepare them for the focus group discussion. The items should include the current policy, if one exists, and a synthesis of the data you have collected about the learning community using Tool 2, Identifying Resources in Your Community, and Tool 3, Identifying Learner Characteristics. Give the date, place, and time for the meeting and request a response within a stated period of time (by telephone, by e-mail, in person, or by letter).

The Amherst H. Wilder Foundation has an excellent manual on conducting focus groups that expands on what we are suggesting. Among the crucial points for success are generating key questions, selecting an experienced facilitator (if possible), creating a script that keeps the session on track, and recording and summarizing what was discussed.

Some key questions when revising an existing policy might be

- What do you believe are the learner-centered strengths of the current policy?
- What improvements would make the current policy more learner-centered?

If a policy does not exist and you are beginning from scratch, you could pose the following questions:

- What are some of the things you look for when working with a library media center collection?
- How can our collection and access services help you meet student standards?

The discussion generated by such questions will enable your focus group to move to the next step, in which you set a vision for learner-centered policy and establish an initial set of broad goals.

STEP 4
Set Strategic Vision and Goals

By the time you begin step 4, you will have considered how to seek advice from critical stakeholders. The tasks listed below could be included in the agenda of your initial focus group session if there is time, or they could form the agenda for a later session. In the latter event, we urge you to summarize what you learned in the initial focus group and route that to the participants in advance of a second meeting.

The principal tasks of step 4 include

1. Setting a strategic vision for the learner-centered collection that is related to the accomplishments of students
2. Identifying broad goals that will guide collection decisions to accomplish your vision (The focus group should consider alternative courses of action for collecting and accessing resources and finalize the goals by reaching a consensus.)
3. Forming a small policy-writing team
4. Developing communication strategies that will be used to test the ideas in the draft policy

Tool 4, Preparing a Strategic Learner-Centered Vision and Collection Goals, shown partially completed in figure 3.4, provides a limited but basic approach that the school library media specialist can use with the focus group in preparing the broad learner-centered goals that will be shared with the learning community (or a subset of the community) and included in the initial draft policy.

Date <u>9/7/05</u>

1. My vision for the library media center is

> The school library serves as the learning center of the school.

2. My three goals for achieving the vision are

> *Goal 1:* To provide physical access to information through a carefully and systematically organized local collection of diverse learning resources that takes into account student learning characteristics and local standards.

> *Goal 2:*

> *Goal 3:*

2. The collection objectives for each of my goals are

> *Goal 1, Objective 1:* To supply 75% of all requested titles to support local reading and literacy standards for grade 2 within 24 hours and to supply 95% within one week, by January 1, 2006.

> *Goal 2, Objective 1:*

> *Goal 3, Objective 1:*

FIGURE 3.4

Partially Completed Version of Tool 4, Preparing a Strategic Learner-Centered Vision and Collection Goals

It is important to remember that you cannot expect most of your stakeholders to remain active throughout each step of the planning process and all the iterations of policy development. You will need to develop a small subcommittee of stakeholders to work with you in actually writing a draft policy that others can respond to. The subcommittee should be formed after you hold the first focus group so that you can plan how to use the information from that meeting.

In table 3.2, we indicated that subject analysis should be part of policy. In chapter 4 we offer more specific advice about how to accomplish that and introduce Tool 8, an additional tool for opening a discussion on the depth, intensity, and currency of current collection subject holdings.

STEP 5
Prepare First Draft of Policy

Begin by preparing a written draft of the policy. Develop appropriate vocabulary and become familiar with the language of policy. This is not difficult in the current environment. Some of the basic texts on collection development include sample policies or parts of policies. Many policies for various types of libraries are available on the Web. Sample policies may also be found in some of the resources recommended at the conclusion of this chapter, and the American Library Association's *Workbook for Selection Policy Writing* (1996) can be extremely helpful. As you read through sample policies, think "learner-centered" and use the language of the elements we have discussed here and that you recorded on the tools you completed. As you are working, make an outline and check it with the elements of policy presented earlier in this chapter.

Essential tasks to be completed in step 5 include

1. Becoming familiar with the essential elements and language of policy documents
2. Deciding which elements should be in your policy
3. Setting a timeline for the first draft
4. Preparing the first draft

You may decide to prepare the policy draft alone or choose a small team to assist you. Your choice depends on the size of your school, the time you have available, and your comfort with the drafting process. In a large and complex setting, you may have to bring in two or three of your stakeholders to work as a writing team under your guidance.

STEP 6
Test Draft of Policy

Once you have completed a draft of your policy, it will be time to test it with a small group of stakeholders. Ask your readers to evaluate your draft by filling in Tool 5, Learner-Centered Policy Critique (shown in figure 3.5). At this point you want to ensure that the major areas are included and that they relate to the learner. Compare your policy to the state or local standards that learners must

	Included	Not Included	Relates to Learner	What Is Needed to Make It Learner-Centered
Introduction (philosophy and mission)				
Goals and objectives				
Selection • Who • What • How				
Collection description/ subject analysis				
Maintenance • Why • When • Criteria applied • How performed				
Evaluation • When • Purpose • Method				
Cooperative (partnerships, networking, and resource sharing)				
Intellectual freedom statement				
Appendixes • Process for reconsideration • Confidentiality statement • ALA Council policies (as appropriate)				

If I were to amend this policy, I would

1. Talk to the following three people:

2. Add the following to make this policy correspond to nationally suggested essential components:

FIGURE 3.5

Tool 5, Learner-Centered Policy Critique

meet to make sure that you have included the necessary resource elements. Such a comparison will enable you to discover what must still be done to clarify how the policy creates a desirable environment for meeting the school's learning goals.

Tool 5 ends with two further steps: identifying people who should be contacted to discuss the policy and identifying additions needed to ensure that the policy includes all of the nationally suggested components.

STEP 7
Revise Policy

Analyze and synthesize the responses provided by your learning community in Step 6. Work with your small writing team to prepare a revision based on what you learned from the analysis of Tool 5 data.

STEP 8
Gain Approval of Policy

Policy does not go into effect until individuals with responsibility for the organization have examined it and agreed on its content. This step is usually carried out well beyond the local school level and requires the signatures of individuals in positions of authority for the institution or for the district in which the institution resides. In the public sector, the local board of education is often responsible for the actions of the library media center. In the private sector, members of the board of directors may be the responsible parties. We suggest the school library media specialist and the principal organize the policy approval path together, with the school library media specialist supplying any information needed by the principal to gain approval.

STEP 9
Communicate and Celebrate

Celebrate! Celebrate! Celebrate! Use all the existing modes of communication to share your learner-centered policy development story. If you have a newsletter, let your readers know how your policy was created and who shared in its development. Highlight the main points that have made it truly learner-centered. Call attention to how your collection and materials access services will enable students, teachers, parents, and caregivers to meet local, state, and national standards. Post the policy where all can see and read it.

The beauty of gaining policy approval is multifaceted. Remember, policy acts as a communication tool for your local community. It explains your collection and access goals, how you make material and access decisions, how you spend your community's funds to support its educational programs, and with whom you cooperate to guide decisions about resource access. And it shows that you understand the library media center's role in the education of learners in your community.

Conclusion

In developing a learner-centered collection policy, your concern is with how your local learning community and learner analysis affect the elements of policy. Clear guidelines, as expressed in policy, are essential for looking closely at learners' developmental, social, and intellectual levels as predictors for selection and access criteria.

The initial step in policy development comes from a clear and detailed description of the community to be served. Once strategies for community and learner analysis are in place, the local school library media specialist can work with our nine-step process to ensure that policy be continually revised to meet curriculum and assessment changes in the local community. Remember that policy is not written in stone. As the learner's world and the relevant information world continue to change, policy revisions must be considered.

NOTES

1. See, for example, Anderson (1996) and Nelson (2001).
2. See, for example, Van Orden and Bishop (2001), Kachel (1997), and Evans (2000).
3. SWOT analysis is a tool that can be used by an organization and its stakeholders. It is most often suggested for scanning both the internal and the external environments for planning purposes. Additional information about SWOT analysis can be found at Mind Tools—Decision Making and Analytical Techniques—SWOT Analysis (http://www.psywww.com/msite/swot.html/).
4. The information found in the completed version of Tool 2 was contributed by a school library media specialist working in a predominantly Hispanic middle school located in North Philadelphia. The information found in the completed version of Tool 3 was contributed by a school library media specialist working in an elementary school in New York City as part of the Robin Hood Library Initiative Project.

RECOMMENDED PROFESSIONAL RESOURCES

American Association of School Librarians. 1999. *A Planning Guide for Information Power: Building Partnerships for Learning.* Chicago: American Library Association.

American Library Association Office for Intellectual Freedom. 1996. *Workbook for Selection Policy Writing.* http://www.ala.org/ala/oif/challengesupport/dealing/workbookselection.htm/ (accessed June 1, 2004).

Anderson, Joanne S., ed. 1996. *Guide for Written Collection Policy Statements.* 2nd ed. Chicago: American Library Association.

Evans, G. Edward. 2000. *Developing Library and Information Center Collections.* 4th ed. Englewood, CO: Libraries Unlimited.

Kachel, Debra E. 1997. *Collection Assessment and Management for School Libraries: Preparing for Cooperative Collection Development.* Westport, CT: Greenwood.

Nelson, Sandra. 2001. *The New Planning for Results: A Streamlined Approach.* Chicago: American Library Association.

Simon, Judith Sharken. 1999. *Conducting Successful Focus Groups.* St. Paul, MN: Amherst H. Wilder Foundation.

Van Orden, Phyllis J., and Kay Bishop. 2001. *The Collection Program in Schools.* 3rd ed. Englewood, CO: Libraries Unlimited.

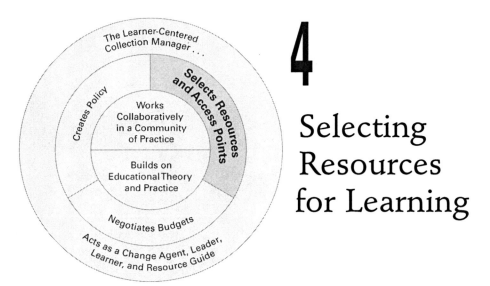

The Learner-Centered Collection Manager . . .

Creates Policy

Selects Resources and Access Points

Works Collaboratively in a Community of Practice

Builds on Educational Theory and Practice

Negotiates Budgets

Acts as a Change Agent, Leader, Learner, and Resource Guide

4

Selecting Resources for Learning

A s we discussed in chapter 1, collection development in a learner-centered environment involves creating a Collaborative Access Environment—identifying resources that match the needs and requirements of the learning community and making those resources available to learners. Sometimes this may entail actually purchasing resources, at other times it may necessitate making resources available through community partners, and at still other times it may involve organizing Internet resources in a way that enables learners to access and use them. Regardless of how the resources are made available, the process of selection is involved.

Tool 6, shown in figure 4.1, presents a decision-making model for selecting resources and access points that support learning. In this model, the needs and requirements of the learning community are the driving force for selection. Resources are made available if they address the information needs of the learning community, match learner characteristics, fit the teaching-learning context, and are consistent with the current knowledge base. As the model indicates, if the resources' costs are within the parameters of the budget, the school library media specialist purchases the resources for the collection. If the costs are too high, the school library media specialist reaches out to partners in the community and makes the resources available in that way when possible.

When developing a learner-centered collection or selecting resources for learning, school library media specialists draw on a range of knowledge, including information about the specific context, the world of resources (print, nonprint, and electronic), and the availability of resources in the broader community.

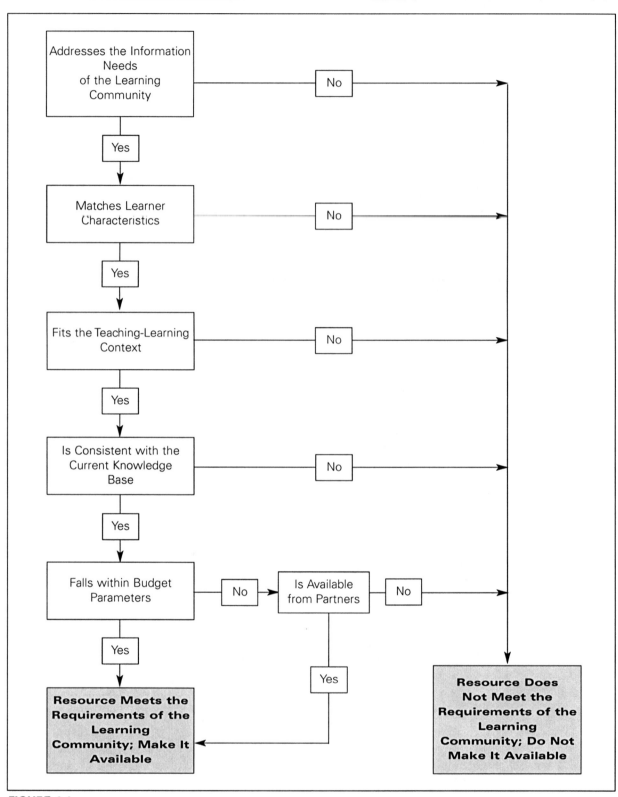

FIGURE 4.1

Tool 6, Decision-Making Model for Selecting Resources and Access Points
That Support Learning

Understanding the Context

One of the most important tasks facing school library media specialists who are creating a learner-centered collection is developing an understanding of their specific context. This includes comprehension of the learners, the teaching-learning context, and the strengths and weaknesses of the current collection.

The Learners

The learners include all the members of the school community: the students, the teachers, the administrators, the parents, and the caregivers. Socioeconomic data describing the broad characteristics of those individuals should be available and can provide one frame of reference for resource and access decisions. More detailed information, such as reading level, writing level, language differences, learning styles, ethnic and cultural background, learning differences, and reading preferences, can provide another frame of reference.

Tool 3, Identifying Learner Characteristics, discussed in detail in chapter 3, provides a matrix for identifying learner characteristics and suggests potential sources of data. Strategies for collecting data about learners include

Using existing demographic data

Using existing test data

Interviewing key informants—administrators, teachers, students, parents, counselors, and other school personnel

Holding focus group sessions with administrators, teachers, students, parents, counselors, and other school personnel

Observing in classrooms

Surveying teachers, parents, administrators, and students

Once the data about the learning community are collected, they need to be analyzed to determine what they tell about the learners you serve and the resources needed to support their learning. For example, if the data indicate that 25 percent of the learners are children of foreign dignitaries who speak English as a second language, then you will need to select resources written in a number of languages and representing a range of cultures. If the data show that 10 percent of the ninth graders are reading at a fifth-grade level, not only will you need to use selection tools that include resources for reluctant readers, such as the Young Adult Library Services Association's "Quick Picks for Reluctant Readers," but you will also need to make information available visually and auditorily through resources such as videos, CD-ROMs, websites, and audiotapes.

The Teaching-Learning Context

In order to develop a learner-centered collection, it is critical for school library media specialists to understand the teaching-learning context, including the community's educational philosophy and the curriculum.

THE COMMUNITY'S EDUCATIONAL PHILOSOPHY

As we discussed in chapter 1, research on how people learn has led many educators to adopt a constructivist philosophy of teaching and learning. Table 4.1, adapted from Lambert (2003), summarizes the principles guiding current educational practice.

Constructivism has far-reaching implications for library programs and library collections. In constructivist settings,

The school library media specialist is the school's resource guide

Learner characteristics and needs are the key issues that guide selection

Access to a breadth of ideas is expected, including ideas in primary resources

Access to information in every format is critical

Access to virtual worlds expands the quantity and quality of information delivery

The library collects the "most appropriate" materials

Resources may be collected "just in time" to meet the ongoing and changing demands of the teaching-learning context

TABLE 4.1

Current Teaching and Learning Principles

Knowledge and beliefs are formed within the learner through interactions with ideas, objects, and people.
The values and beliefs of learners affect how they interpret and assign meaning to their experiences.
Learning activities should allow learners to use what they know to interpret new information and to construct new knowledge.
Culture, race, and economic status affect student learning both in and out of school.
Learning is a social activity that is enhanced by shared inquiry.
Learning requires students to reflect on their own learning.
Learners are partners in the assessment process.
The outcomes of learning are varied and often unpredictable.

Source: Adapted from Linda Lambert, *Leadership Capacity for Lasting School Improvement* (Alexandria, VA: Association for Supervision and Curriculum Development, 2003), p. 59.

THE CURRICULUM

During the last decade the standards movement has influenced curriculum development across the country. National standards, such as those developed by the National Council of Teachers of Mathematics or the National Council of Teachers of English, provide a vision and a unifying conceptual structure to different disciplines. State and local content benchmarks for certain grade levels (such as grades 4, 8, and 12) extend national standards to provide a local curriculum framework, thus leading to better definition of the important ideas to be included in the curriculum and smoother articulation from grade to grade. Most curriculum designs at the state and local levels have resulted in a narrowing and deepening of the curriculum, with an emphasis on in-depth understanding rather than broad coverage.

While the standards movement has led to clarity in curriculum expectations, the translation of standards to actual teaching and learning still rests with individual teachers and thus varies from school to school and from classroom to classroom. In addition, the estimated number of families homeschooling their children has grown dramatically in the last decade. While many families who choose to homeschool their children use local or state curricula, others rely on curricula developed especially for homeschoolers, and still others create their own.

In order to develop a library collection that supports the curriculum, then, a school library media specialist must have a clear picture of the enacted curriculum, or the curriculum that is actually taught in the course of an academic year, including

- Major subjects and topics
- State and local standards or benchmarks
- Essential questions that focus instruction and assessment
- Skills and processes
- Teaching methods
- Assessment strategies and end products
- Classroom organization

Tool 7, Matrix for Gathering Data about the Curriculum,[1] provides a format for collecting data about a school's curriculum. Strategies for gathering such data include

- Observing in classrooms
- Participating on curriculum and technology committees
- Analyzing local curriculum documentation
- Reviewing state and local academic standards
- Analyzing student work
- Conducting teacher and student surveys

A partially completed version of Tool 7 is shown in figure 4.2. The Virginia Standards of Learning were used as the basis for completing the tool.[2]

After each teacher or grade level has completed Tool 7, the data can be combined to develop a schoolwide curriculum map—a graphic representation of the

Teacher __Mrs. Murphy__ Grade _6_ Subject __Science__

Month	Content	Standards or Benchmarks	Skills and Processes	Assessment Strategy/ End Product
September	Force, motion, and energy—basic sources of energy, their origins, transformations, and uses	6.2	Compare and contrast potential and kinetic energy through common examples found in the natural environment Compare and contrast renewable and nonrenewable energy resources	Create a model of an energy transformation Design an investigation that demonstrates light energy being transformed into other forms of energy
October	Force, motion, and energy—role of solar system in driving most natural processes within the atmosphere, the hydrosphere, and on the Earth's surface	6.3	Comprehend and apply basic terminology related to solar energy Analyze and explain how convection currents occur	Model and explain the greenhouse effect
November	Matter—structure and role of atoms; characteristics of water and its role in a human-made environment	6.4, 6.5	Compare and contrast the atomic structure of two different elements Explain that elements are represented by symbols	Create and interpret a simplified model of the structure of an atom Design an investigation to determine the effects of heat on the states of water

FIGURE 4.2

Partially Completed Version of Tool 7, Matrix for Gathering Data about the Curriculum

content, skills, processes, and assessment strategies used by all the teachers in a building during the course of a school year. Specific details for constructing curriculum maps are beyond the scope of this book but can be found in a number of resources, including *The Information-Powered School* (Hughes-Hassell and Wheelock 2001) and *Mapping the Big Picture: Integrating Curriculum and Assessment K–12* (Jacobs 1997).

Using a curriculum map, the school library media specialist can identify

• The types and number of resources needed to support learning

• When, how, and where learners need access

• Utility software and other technology needed to complete assessment products

• Budget needs for resources to support the curriculum

Two examples demonstrate how understanding the community's educational philosophy and the curriculum inform collection development.

Example 1. Many schools that adhere to a constructivist approach to education use Howard Gardner's theory of multiple intelligences (MI) as an organizing framework for learning. According to Gardner's theory, intelligence is a plurality of capacities, each of which is brought to bear on learning and problem solving across the disciplines.[3] Table 4.2 shows how using MI as the organizing framework for literacy development affects the types of resources you select and make available to learners.[4]

Example 2. While reviewing the curriculum, a school library media specialist discovers that the topic "magnets" is studied in kindergarten and then again in fourth grade. In kindergarten, students are expected to investigate and understand the key concepts of attraction/nonattraction, push/pull, attract/repel, and metal/nonmetal as well as useful applications of magnets, such as in refrigerator

TABLE 4.2

Multiple Intelligences and the Selection of Literacy Resources

Intelligence	*Characteristics of Resources*
Linguistic	Demonstrate the beauty and power of the written word (for example, books on tape or videotapes of poetry, short stories, or novels; guest storytellers and poets)
Bodily-kinesthetic	Allow students to physically interact with them (for example, software programs that allow students to interact with text by making notations, manipulating bookmarks, and putting sticky notes on favorite passages)
Spatial	Allow visual interaction (for example, pop-up books, three-dimensional books, and books that come apart into puzzle pieces and can be reconstructed)
Musical	Include songs, rhymes, raps, alliteration (for example, CDs, videos, software, and websites that focus on the rhythmic nature of language)
Logical-mathematical	Focus on numbers (for example, online databases and websites that present sports statistics or recipes)
Intrapersonal	Deal directly with emotions and emotionally charged issues such as racism, sexual abuse, and drug use (for example, nonfiction resources that deal specifically with feelings)
Interpersonal	Demonstrate the power youth have to affect social change (for example, websites that provide opportunities for students to interact in writing with others who are interested in social action and change)
Natural	Appeal to those that are naturalistically inclined (for example, nature guides, maps, and field guides to specific regions, parks, or landmarks)

magnets, magnetized screwdrivers, and magnetic games. In fourth grade, students expand their understanding of magnets to include electromagnets and their role in producing electricity. Students are expected to be able to create a diagram of a magnetic field using a magnet, compare and contrast a permanent magnet and an electromagnet, explain how electricity is generated by a moving magnetic field, and construct a simple electronic magnet using a wire, nail, or other iron-bearing object and a dry cell. Obviously, the resources required to support student learning about magnets in each of the grades would be quite different. The school library media specialist's job of analyzing the current collection to assess its responsiveness to the needs of students learning about magnets in kindergarten and in fourth grade, as well as searching for new resources, is made easier with the information gleaned from the curriculum map.

Strengths and Weaknesses of the Current Collection

Understanding the strengths and weaknesses of the current collection is basic to meeting the unique needs of your learners. Our purpose in this section, however, is not to repeat how-to instructions for collection analysis that can be found easily elsewhere. For example, *Managing and Analyzing Your Collection* (Doll and Barron 2002) and *Building a School Collection Plan: A Beginning Handbook with Internet Assist* (Loertscher, Woolls, and Felker 1998) provide step-by-step instructions for gathering and analyzing the current collection. Instead, our purpose is to call attention to the need for collection analysis to focus on how well the collection meets the needs of learners and supports the teaching-learning context.

We are suggesting that school library media specialists who are developing a learner-centered collection need to expand their analysis beyond standard questions such as "Are the items in predicted high-use curriculum areas dated?" or "Do I need replacements for items in poor condition or with obsolete information?" to include the following questions that assess how well the resources match learner characteristics and support the teaching-learning context:

How well do the items support the learning styles of my learners (visual, auditory, bodily-kinesthetic)?

How well do the items support the reading levels of my learners?

How well do the items support the learning differences of my learners?

How well do the items reflect the ethnic diversity of my community?

How well do the items support attainment of curricular standards or benchmarks?

How well do the items support large-group, small-group, and individual work?

How well do the items help students create the expected student product (for example, a PowerPoint slide show with video clips)?

Answering these types of questions requires school library media specialists to modify the qualitative and quantitative approaches for collection analysis they normally use. In the next two sections, we offer suggestions on how both approaches might be altered to demonstrate how your library supports the specific needs of learners. We suggest using Tool 8, Collection Development Analysis Worksheet, to record your assessment of the current collection and its responsiveness to curricular priorities, to indicate where policy changes are needed, and to provide directions to your vendor. Tool 8 can be used to provide data that broadly indicate how deeply the library media center holds materials for each Dewey decimal classification area and in what formats. It also provides an opportunity for the school library media specialist to work collaboratively with teachers and other stakeholders to focus collection decisions on specific learner characteristics and curricular needs. An example of a completed Tool 8 is presented in figure 4.3.

QUALITATIVE TECHNIQUES

We recognize that standard library practice suggests collection evaluation by list checking your holdings against authoritative resources such as *The Elementary School Library Collection* (Homa et al. 2000) or *Senior High School Library Catalog* (2002). This type of collection examination is based on the belief that a collection should be held against an authoritative bibliographic tool containing recommended titles. The assumption is that the more items in the collection that are recommended from an authoritative list, the better the collection.

Learner-centered practice, however, suggests a variation of this approach. Selection aides that we mention below, such as Peterson's *Literary Pathways: Selecting Books to Support New Readers* (2001), are not part of the basic lists suggested for collection analysis, but they can be helpful in analyzing the ability of the collection to support early literacy development. Aiming for a percentage of holdings from Peterson's list could be helpful in determining buying strategies. Consulting the school district's adopted reading series and conferring with both the reading specialist and the grade-level teachers will also provide insight into the strengths and weaknesses of the collection in relation to the school's literacy goals.

QUANTITATIVE METHODS

Gathering quantitative data about a collection has become more possible as libraries are automated and circulation systems are capable of generating reports on variables such as the number of items in an area, the age of a subject area, and circulation patterns within specific subject codes. For collections that are not automated, a tool exists that enables the school library media specialist to generate a random sample of the collection and analyze it for the above variables as well as others. Readers should consult *Dr. Drott's Random Sampler* (Drott 1996), a web-based tool that explains sampling and takes readers through the sampling process based on the size of their collections.

Quantitative collection analysis techniques can point to

> The number of items in a collection in a specific Dewey or Library of Congress (LC) classification area. Even a rough count of items has an impact on what can be made available to learners.

SUBJECT FIELD		COLLECTION DESCRIPTION				POLICY	SELECTION PROFILE			
Dewey	Description	Current Impact Level*	Median Age	Comments/ Special Notes**	Proposed Impact Level*	Responsibility: Gifts, Evaluation, Weeding	Format	Variables: Language, Geography, Chronological Period, etc.	Publisher	Price
Easy	Caldecott Award books	1	1960	Third-graders study Caldecott Award Missing recent titles	3	Caldecott Award lists consulted	Books, DVDs, videos, books on tape	English, Spanish	—	$640
Fiction	Transition novels, series books	1	1968	New reading series adopted Titles needed	2	Reading series/ reading teacher consulted Reviews collected for additions	Permabound, paperback, hardback, books on tape	English, Spanish	—	$6,500
Ref. 000	Encyclopedias	1	1975	New state assessment Encyclopedias needed to support research component	2	Reviews collected for additions	Print, electronic	English	Indicate specific publishers	$755

* Impact Level
  1 = minimum support
  2 = adequate support
  3 = enhanced support

** Comments/Special Notes
  • Curricular priorities
  • Standards addressed
  • Condition of materials

FIGURE 4.3

Completed Version of Tool 8, Collection Development Analysis Worksheet

The age of the collection according to Dewey or LC classification areas. This gives the collection manager a general picture of the currency of thought, or lack of it, that exists in items within the collection.

The circulation patterns for materials within Dewey or LC classification areas. This indicates the degree of usage, or nonusage, that various topics are experiencing.

The condition of the collection within Dewey or LC classification areas. Condition has several implications. If materials are in excellent condition in a subject area, one wonders whether they are experiencing any usage. On the other hand, materials that are in poor condition could indicate an area in which items should be checked for removal or reordering. Users rarely pull items in poor condition from the shelves, even if those items are sufficiently current and potentially useful.

To evaluate condition and to assess how well the materials match learner characteristics and support the teaching-learning context, on-site examination of sample items is needed.

Understanding the World of Resources

Keeping up with new resources, advances in online searching, and changes in technology and delivery mechanisms is a necessary component of learner-centered selection. Sources of information about the changing world of resources include selection criteria, selection tools, and the role of the learning community in selection.

Selection Criteria

Many authors have discussed in detail the general selection criteria that may be applied to all types of materials.[5] The most common general selection criteria are summarized in table 4.3.

In developing a learner-centered collection, the same basic selection criteria apply; however, the emphasis in all selection decisions is on whether the resources match learner characteristics and address the teaching-learning context. This means that certain criteria, such as appropriateness, scope, treatment, and arrangement, become more central to the decision-making process, while other criteria, such as literary quality, reputation of the author or illustrator, aesthetic quality, and physical quality, may become less important. In other words, selection shifts from purchasing "the best" to purchasing the "most appropriate." While at first this may sound like heresy, if we remember that we are buying resources not "just in case" but rather to better serve *our specific learners* "just in time," then the shift seems natural.

A second shift involves the picture of the child or student we hold in our head as we examine a resource or read a review. Often, when making selection

TABLE 4.3

General Selection Criteria

INTELLECTUAL CONTENT	
Criteria	*Description*
Authority	Addresses the qualifications and abilities of the people who created the work
Appropriateness	Addresses the suitability of the content for the intended audience
Scope	Refers to the author's purpose for the work and the overall breadth and depth of the coverage
Accuracy	Refers to the currency, correctness, and perspective of the information
Treatment	Deals with the style of presentation and whether it is appropriate for the subject, genre, and user's developmental level; addresses multicultural elements and stereotyping where appropriate
Arrangement and organization	Focuses on the sequence and development of ideas and how they facilitate comprehension of the material; addresses how easily information can be located
Literary merit	Refers to how well the author and illustrator deal with literary components
Reputation of author, illustrator, or producer	Refers to the contributions of the author or illustrator
PHYSICAL FORMAT	
Criteria	*Description*
Physical quality	Refers to elements such as clarity of images, illustrations, speech, and music; consistency of navigation icons; legibility of typeface or fonts; and navigation
Aesthetic quality	Addresses the aesthetic appeal of the work
OTHER CONSIDERATIONS	
Criteria	*Description*
Series	Refers to the quality of books and other materials that are part of a series
Comparison with other works	Focuses on how the work compares with others by the same author or illustrator or on the same topic

decisions we think about whether the resource will meet the needs of the typical child—the average seventh grader, for instance. In developing a learner-centered collection, it is essential to think about the *specific* learners, recognizing that in the seventh grade, for example, there may be learners representing a range of intellectual, social, and emotional levels; reading levels; learning styles; learning and language differences; and cultural and ethnic backgrounds. And in today's educational climate, all of those learners, regardless of who they are, will be expected to master the same content standards and will need resources to support their learning.

Three concrete examples help clarify our points.

Example 1. Research in emergent literacy tells us that children who are learning to read need access to books with specific features, including familiar oral language patterns, repeated phrases, patterned stories, illustrations depicting the message in written text, and links to readers' prior knowledge. A large percentage of the books that meet those criteria are referred to as little books. Such books, written especially for emergent readers, are published by companies like Rigby, Wright Group, and Mondo. The authors of little books are seldom well-known to children's literature experts, and the books themselves are rarely listed in *Books in Print* or reviewed in periodicals like *School Library Journal* (Reed Business). If little books were evaluated primarily on their literary quality, physical quality, and aesthetic appeal, many school library media specialists would not deem them worthy of including in a library collection. However, if they are evaluated first and foremost on their appropriateness, scope, treatment, and arrangement, they become critical purchases for elementary-school library collections and public library collections serving children in the primary grades.

Example 2. Many school systems have adopted the Core Knowledge Sequence, a curriculum for preschool to grade 8 that offers a shared and coherent sequence of specific knowledge in the content areas. E. D. Hirsch, the founder of the Core Knowledge Foundation, and his colleagues have developed recommended lists of resources to support the Core Knowledge curriculum. Many of those resources would be overlooked by school library media specialists who are focused on purchasing "the best." The Core Classic Series, for example, which contains abridged versions of classic works like *The Legend of Sleepy Hollow* and *Don Quixote*, would not meet most school library media specialists' standards for literary quality or aesthetic appeal.

Example 3. When seeking to support the science curriculum, a school library media specialist focused on selecting resources for the typical middle-school student might not think about purchasing nonfiction picture books, books on tape, or nonfiction trade books labeled for beginning readers. The availability of such resources, however, may be essential to the success of students with learning differences or learning difficulties.

In learner-centered selection, then, the foremost shift is in which selection criteria receive primary consideration and on the questions you ask yourself when examining resources. The focus is always on how well a resource meets the needs of the specific learner and supports the teaching-learning context. Table 4.4 summarizes the learner-centered selection criteria and questions we are suggesting.

Selection Tools

Selection tools, such as reviewing journals and professionally recommended lists, are a mainstay of the school library media specialist's trade. School library

TABLE 4.4

Learner-Centered Selection Criteria

PRIMARY CONSIDERATIONS	
Criteria	*Questions to Consider*
Appropriateness	Is the content appropriate for my learners?
	Does it match their developmental level? reading level? social development? learning style? ethnic or cultural background?
	Will the work be of interest to my learners?
Scope	What is the purpose of the work?
	Is the level of detail appropriate for my learners?
	Does it support the school curriculum or interests of the students?
Accuracy	Is the material up-to-date and accurate?
	Are opinions and biases, if they exist, acknowledged as such?
	Does the creator of the work identify the sources used to create it?
	Does the creator cite credible sources, including specialists or experts in the subject area?
Treatment	Is the style of presentation appropriate for the subject matter and does it have appeal to my learners?
	Does the creator avoid stereotypes dealing with race, gender, age, region, and socioeconomic level?
	Does the resource reflect our diverse society?
Arrangement and organization	Is the information arranged and organized so that students can understand it?
	Is the resource organized so that students can easily locate information?
Authority	What are the creator's qualifications?
	How knowledgeable is the creator about the subject?
	Does the creator cite credible sources, including specialists or experts in the subject area?
	Has the creator published or produced other materials on this topic?
Comparison with other works	How does this work compare with others in the same genre and format or on the same subject?
	How might my learners use this work?
	How might educators use it with students?

TABLE 4.4

Learner-Centered Selection Criteria (cont.)

SECONDARY CONSIDERATIONS	
Criteria	*Questions to Consider*
Physical quality	Do physical elements such as the clarity of images, illustrations, speech, and music, the consistency of navigation icons, and the legibility of typefaces or fonts support the purpose of the work and the learning styles of my learners?
Aesthetic quality	Will the work appeal to the aesthetic tastes of my learners?
Literary merit	How well does the author, illustrator, or producer deal with literary components such as theme, setting, character, and style?
Reputation of author, illustrator, or producer	Do my learners use other works by this individual and would they find this title interesting and worthwhile?

media specialists working in a learner-centered environment must remember four things about selection tools:

1. Selection tools featuring reviews that merely focus on plot summaries, that use vague language, or that turn into showcases for the reviewers' writing skills hamper your ability to do your job. Reviews need to examine materials assertively—to provide levels of analysis, comparison with other materials, and evaluation that make it possible for you to determine the value of a resource to your students.

2. Since literary quality is not the sole determinant of a purchasing decision, perhaps the most valuable part of a review is information that places the resource in context. How does the resource compare with others of the same genre, in the same format, or on the same subject? How might children use the resource, and how can it be used in your work with children? In what type of collection would the resource be of value? Is the resource a necessary purchase?

3. The range of resources you use for selection must be broad. While standard selection tools will still prove useful, you may need to expand your search to include lesser-known resources or those marketed primarily for teachers or for parents. For example, school library media specialists purchasing resources to support early literacy development will want to consult journals such as *Reading Teacher* (International Reading Association) and *Language Arts* (National Council of Teachers of English) and books such as *Literary Pathways: Selecting Books to Support New Readers* (Peterson 2001) and *Matching Books to Readers: Using Leveled Books in Guided Reading K–3* (Fountas and Gay 1999). School library media specialists working in communities with diverse ethnic populations will find help in such resources as the Barahona Center for the Study of Books in Spanish for Children and Adolescents (http://www.csusm.edu/csb/),

Oyate: A Native Organization (http://www.oyate.org/), and the Black Books Galore series (http://www.blackbooksgalore.com/).

4. Selection tools should not be used as substitutes for local judgment. Just because review X claims that an item is great does not mean that it fits your local needs. The data you have collected about your learners and about the teaching-learning context allow you to evaluate the utility of a resource for your particular setting.

The Role of the Learning Community in Selection

Building a collaborative access environment demands that school library media specialists, teachers, and other members of the learning community enter into a collaborative relationship and share authority for collection and access decisions. As we discussed in chapter 2, school library media specialists need to acknowledge and welcome the expertise that other members of the learning community, including students, bring to the table concerning electronic resources, delivery mechanisms, and even print resources. Using Tool 1, Stakeholder Contact/SWOT Analysis, discussed in detail in chapter 3, school library media specialists can identify all the members of the learning community that should be involved in the selection process.

Strategies for involving teachers and students in the selection process include conducting interest inventories with students; routing reviewing journals to teachers; attending faculty, departmental, or grade-level meetings to elicit input and discuss future purchases; routing bibliographies to teachers; and forming an advisory committee. Weblogs too provide a natural avenue for communicating with the wider learning community about collection development and for soliciting others' input.

Understanding the Resources in the Community

In today's information-rich world, no individual school library can contain all the resources and information learners need to be successful. Technology is a primary tool for connecting learners with local, district, regional, and even global resources. Knowing what resources are available in the broader community and integrating them into the collection are key components of selection for school library media specialists creating a collaborative access environment.

Tool 2, Identifying Resources in Your Community, first introduced in chapter 3, can be used to determine the types of resources, both human and material, that are available from organizations, businesses, and other institutions in your community. The public library and local university library, for example, are natural partners for school libraries. Memberships in state or regional consortia provide students with access to electronic magazines, encyclopedias, atlases, and other reference materials. Community-based organizations, like local education funds, provide support for efforts to connect businesses, museums, and other community agencies and their resources to the community's students.

Access to the World Wide Web has also expanded the range of resources available from the broader community. The challenge for collectors, as well as for users, becomes separating the wheat from the chaff. Many authors provide guidelines for evaluating websites.[6] Again, it is important to remember that in addition to such criteria, you must consider the needs and requirements of the learning community when selecting Internet resources. Ask yourself:

Is the website of interest to my learners?

Does the website support the school curriculum or the interests of my learners?

Is the content appropriate for my learners? Does it match their developmental level? reading level? social development? learning style? ethnic or cultural background?

Is the level of detail appropriate for my learners?

How might my learners use the website?

How might educators use the website with students?

Conclusion

In this chapter we have challenged some of the sacred cows associated with selection. For example:

We used to believe that selection was the sole responsibility of the school library media specialist. We now know that collection development must become a shared process.

We used to believe that our job was to collect the best resources just in case. We now know that our job is to collect the most appropriate resources and to reserve funds for just-in-time purchases.

We used to believe that expert judgment should guide selection. We now know that the teaching-learning context and the characteristics of our specific learners dictate what is collected on-site and what is suggested for access. Although reviewers can sort and describe parts of the proliferating information world, they cannot be the primary judges of what should be purchased or made available.

We used to believe that the school library should contain all the resources and information that learners need. We now know that partnerships are critical to the creation of an information-rich environment for learning and that technology plays a key role in connecting learners with resources.

NOTES

1. Additional tools for gathering curriculum data are provided in Heidi Hayes Jacobs (1997), *Mapping the Big Picture: Integrating Curriculum and Assessment K–12,* and Michael B. Eisenberg and Robert E. Berkowitz (1998), *Curriculum Initiative: An Agenda and Strategy for Library Media Programs.*

2. The Commonwealth of Virginia Standards of Learning formed the basis for this matrix. The standards are available at http://www.pen.k12.va.us/VDOE/Superintendent/Sols/home.shtml/.

3. For a complete description of multiple intelligences see Howard Gardner (1983), *Frames of Mind*.

4. See Thomas Armstrong (2003), *The Multiple Intelligences of Reading and Writing: Making the Words Come Alive,* for a detailed discussion of the application of multiple intelligences to literacy development.

5. See, for example, Van Orden and Bishop (2001), Evans (2000), and Van Orden (2000).

6. See, for example, Pam Berger (1998), *Internet for Active Learners: Curriculum-Based Strategies for K–12.*

RECOMMENDED PROFESSIONAL RESOURCES

Armstrong, Thomas. 2003. *The Multiple Intelligences of Reading and Writing: Making the Words Come Alive.* Alexandria, VA: Association of Supervision and Curriculum Development.

Barahona Center for the Study of Books in Spanish for Children and Adolescents. http://www.csusm.edu/csb/ (accessed February 16, 2004).

Berger, Pam. 1998. *Internet for Active Learners: Curriculum-Based Strategies for K–12.* Chicago: American Library Association.

Black Books Galore. http://www.blackbooksgalore.com/ (accessed February 16, 2004).

Books in Print. 2004. New Providence, NJ: R. R. Bowker.

Cervantes Saavedra, Miguel de, and Michael J. Marshall. 1999. *Don Quixote.* Abridged ed. Core Classics Series. Charlottesville, VA: Core Knowledge Foundation.

Doll, Carol A., and Pamela Petrick Barron. 2002. *Managing and Analyzing Your Collection: A Practical Guide for Small Libraries and School Media Centers.* Chicago: American Library Association.

Drott, M. Carl. 1996. *Dr. Drott's Random Sampler.* http://drott.cis.drexel.edu/sample/DrottHome.html/ (accessed February 16, 2004).

Eisenberg, Michael B., and Robert E. Berkowitz. 1998. *Curriculum Initiative: An Agenda and Strategy for Library Media Programs.* Norwood, NJ: Ablex.

Evans, G. Edward. 2000. *Developing Library and Information Center Collections.* 4th ed. Englewood, CO: Libraries Unlimited.

Fountas, Irene, and Gay Su Pinnell. 1999. *Matching Books to Readers: Using Leveled Books in Guided Reading K–3.* Portsmouth, NH: Heinemann.

Gardner, Howard. 1983. *Frames of Mind.* New York: Basic Books.

Homa, Linda L., Ann L. Schreck, and Maureen Hoebener, eds. 2000. *The Elementary School Library Collection: A Guide to Books and Other Media.* 22nd ed. Williamsport, PA: Brodart.

Hughes-Hassell, Sandra, and Anne Wheelock, eds. 2001. *The Information-Powered School.* Chicago: American Library Association.

Irving, Washington. 1999. *The Legend of Sleepy Hollow.* Core Classics Series. Charlottesville, VA: Core Knowledge Foundation.

Jacobs, Heidi Hayes. 1997. *Mapping the Big Picture: Integrating Curriculum and Assessment K–12.* Alexandria, VA: Association for Supervision and Curriculum Development.

Lambert, Linda. 2003. *Leadership Capacity for Lasting School Improvement.* Alexandria, VA: Association for Supervision and Curriculum Development.

Loertscher, David V., Blanche Woolls, and Janice Felker. 1998. *Building a School Collection Plan: A Beginning Handbook with Internet Assist.* San Jose, CA: Hi Willow Research and Publishing.

Oyate: A Native Organization. http://www.oyate.org/ (accessed February 16, 2004).

Peterson, Barbara. 2001. *Literary Pathways: Selecting Books to Support New Readers.* Portsmouth, NH: Heinemann.

Senior High School Library Catalog. 2002.16th ed. New York: H. W. Wilson.

Van Orden, Phyllis J. 2000. *Selecting Books for the Elementary School Library Media Center: A Complete Guide.* New York: Neal-Schuman.

Van Orden, Phyllis J., and Kay Bishop. 2001. *The Collection Program in Schools.* 3rd ed. Englewood, CO: Libraries Unlimited.

Walker, Deborah, and Linda Lambert. 1995. "Learning and Leading Theory: A Century in the Making." In *The Constructivist Leader,* ed. Linda Lambert et al., 1–27. New York: Teachers College Press.

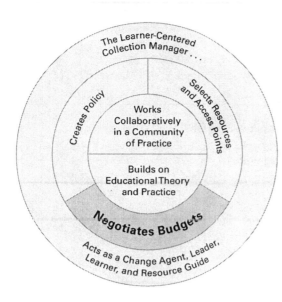

5

Budgeting for Maximum Impact on Learning

In chapter 2 we presented the changing behaviors essential for learner-centered collectors. We identified four roles that affect how the collection manager creates and uses various budgeting techniques to achieve library media center collection and access services that can be categorized as learner-centered:

1. As a resource guide the collector is knowledgeable about the price tag for various formats.
2. As a change agent the collector shares expertise about the cost of needed resources.
3. As a leader the collector develops budgeting techniques that enable him or her to explain resources essential to support specific programs.
4. As a learner the collector continues to modify his or her behavior to meet the financial challenges that are essential to marketing the library media center's role in achieving local, state, and national standards.

In chapter 3 we argued that policy guides the development of procedures for efficiency in collection operations. Learner-centered policy should include statements about how budgeted funds are allocated based on program considerations, including decisions on subject collecting, availability and cost of various material formats, agreements with consortia on resource support, and cooperative agreements between the school and the public library regarding subject collection depth in each institution..

In chapter 4 we presented a decision-making model for selecting resources and access points that support learning. In that model, the needs and requirements of the learning community are the driving force for selection. Resources are made available if they address the information needs of the learning community, match learner characteristics, fit the teaching-learning context, and are consistent with the current knowledge base. As the model indicates, if the resources are within the parameters of the budget, the school library media specialist purchases them for the collection. If they are not, the school library media specialist must negotiate for additional support or reach out to partners in the broader community to make resources available.

In this chapter, we think about the budget as an action plan for maximizing the collection's impact on learning and we consider the behaviors the collector must assume, the elements of policy that must be in place, and the criteria for resource selection that develops learners. Specifically, we

>Describe sources of income and basic budget models so that our readers can determine what the various models can and cannot do to help a library gain sufficient resources for learners

>Illustrate the steps in developing a learner-centered budget with a real-life story about an elementary-school library media specialist who successfully adopted a new model during budgeting and used it to indicate how particular budget requests supported the school's learning priorities

>Look at emerging considerations in developing learner-centered budgets

>Suggest strategies for change to support learner-centered objectives

>Offer tools for creating learner-centered budgeting approaches

>Indicate available professional resources useful for understanding the budgeting process

Sources of Income

In order to budget you have to understand where the funds originate and how you can influence the process. Initially, four questions come to mind:

1. What are the sources of income?
2. How are they received?
3. What does receipt of funding require?
4. What are the spending deadlines?

A diagram showing the basic allocations for school library media centers would probably indicate that the basic source of support for school library media centers comes from the school district. The funds are allocated in various configurations. Funding in the public sector is often determined on a per capita basis; that is, a fixed dollar amount is allocated for each student served. Schools in the private sector may receive per capita funding or may be given a lump sum of money that is based on previous practice and adjusted for anticipated changes, such as inflation. Additional sources of income may include fines, support from parents' or friends' groups, grants, matching funds, gift shop sales, user fees, gifts, donations, and perhaps endowment funds.

It is important to understand what each source of income requires. When most funds come from the general school district, school library media specialists must know how to bargain from year to year to obtain the financial support needed to accomplish their learner-centered library's educational goals. They must tell a compelling story and clearly explain what success will cost.

Basic Budget Models

Your organization may use one or more of the budget models described below. Table 5.1 provides a summary of the advantages, disadvantages, and considerations for each.

The Lump-Sum Budget

As an elementary school library media specialist in an independent school, you may be given a lump-sum budget for materials expenditures. The lump sum is not predicated on the number of students served but rather on previous library expenditures adjusted for inflation and on behind-the-scenes negotiation based on examples of funding from similar schools. With this type of budget it is the school library media specialist's job to decide how the funds are divided for subject and format support, based on the funders' assumption that the specialist has a basic understanding of what is available and what is needed by the school community. No line-item or program documentation may be required.

The lump-sum budget may look attractive but has serious problems. It appears to allow great freedom in how funds are allocated, but in reality there is the unexpressed assumption that monies will be used to support activities as they have been in the past. This type of budgeting does not easily present opportunities to bargain for additional monies or to argue against any reductions that may have been included.

The Line-Item Budget

The most usual budget model is the line-item, or object of expenditure, budget. Within such a budget there will be at least one line for materials and access. Funds are assigned to broad categories, perhaps with separate lines for different material formats and database access. The usual technique is to show the previous year, the current year, and what is projected for the coming year within each line. Again, there is little opportunity to negotiate based on program needs since specific program justification may not be part of this budgeting process.

The Performance Budget

The least useful and perhaps most questionable approach is the performance, or function, budget, which states the unit costs for specific activities that are performed, such as processing materials and other technical services needed to make items available to clientele. Consider the problem in showing the cost for cataloging and processing each library unit to make it ready for collection use. Then imagine the response of the person who is ultimately responsible for your funding when he or she sees how costly it is to process a hardcover item. Potential reaction: buy paperbacks, which are cheaper, and forget any processing costs.

TABLE 5.1

Budgeting Approaches

Approach	Advantages	Disadvantages	Considerations
Lump-Sum Budget	No apparent priorities Establishes a single pot of money	Provides little potential for negotiating Historical assumptions for actions No relationship to learner outcomes	Used only in very small media centers
Line-Item Budget	Usual, best-known, typical model Known categories for funds Identifies support per student	Little opportunity to negotiate within and between lines No relationship to learner outcomes	Typical budget format used Shows per-pupil support that can be used to compare across schools, districts, states, and the nation
Performance Budget	Explains particulars of unit costs for operations	Easily misunderstood since there are no ties to programs No relationship to learner outcomes	Rarely useful and rarely used in school library media budgeting
Program Budget	Collection goals address programs Addresses costs and means to deliver programs Shows number of outputs possible per program	Difficult to adjust resource support across more than one program Shows outputs but no outcomes for learners	Basic program objectives and outputs incorporated in a budget-negotiation document Creates beginning tie of spending to programs
Zero-Based Budget	Collection goals address programs Shows delivery costs for programs at various levels Identifies decision units Presents alternative levels of funding in incremental steps Permits ranking of activities Spells out impacts of various levels of funding	Full ZBB is too time-consuming for school library media center development purposes	Spending activities are tied to program goals Incremental budget levels for achieving goals can be shown
Combination Program and Zero-Based Budget	Collection goals are collaboratively developed with the learning community to address desired learning outcomes Shows delivery costs for programs at various levels Identifies decision units Presents alternative levels of funding in incremental steps Permits ranking of activities Spells out impacts of various levels of funding		Spending activities are tied to program goals Incremental budget levels for achieving goals can be shown Collaborative planning is the heart of budget allocations Collection impact can be related to school learning priorities

The Program Budget

A program budget describes the cost attached to the delivery of various library media programs and services and usually contains a budget under each program description. The idea in program budgeting is to describe both the programs and services and the means to deliver them (staff cost, materials cost, and so forth). Inputs, such as staff time and materials, and outputs, such as total cost and cost per user, are listed. The idea is to see the costs and benefits of various programs, perhaps in order to decide which ones are worth their price for the organization. The problem is that staff and materials can overlap into many different program areas. For example, how do you eliminate one-third of a set of encyclopedias that is used in three programs if one of the programs is slated for elimination? Most important, what does this type of information really tell us about what students are able to do as a result of materials made available to them?

The Zero-Based Budget

In a zero-based budget (ZBB), financial planning starts from a zero base (the base just above opening the doors and turning on the heat and electricity) and projects into the future what it will cost to deliver programs and services at various levels. Alternative budgets are created for ranges from a minimal level to an ideal level of operation. In this case the budget becomes a real planning tool, demonstrating what is possible and what impact could be achieved at various levels of funding. ZBB speaks to an organization's objectives by addressing

> *Effectiveness of spending.* Effectiveness is measured by the extent to which the objectives of the organization are achieved—for example, the extent to which all beginning readers have books available at their reading and development level.
>
> *Efficiency of spending.* Efficiency reflects the economy with which something happens—for example, the cost of making available one book suitable for each beginning reader.
>
> *Alternative funding levels.* Alternatives for any given activity identify what can happen at different levels of financial support—for example, how the cost of developing a book collection for beginning readers in kindergarten and grade 1 varies for levels of support ranging from minimum to maximum.

There is a basic framework for building a ZBB presentation. It includes the following steps:

1. Planning assumptions are developed based on the objectives of the parent organization (the school) and the environmental factors that enter into the picture. Objectives might include student learning goals and state standards that must be met by students in areas such as reading and math. Environmental factors that enter into budgeting include basic material costs and predicted inflation rates for the year under consideration.
2. Decision units, which may include programs, projects, and services, are identified.

3. The decision units are analyzed. This is the heart of ZBB. Within each decision unit objectives, current operations, workload measures, and performance measures are described, and alternatives and incremental analyses are presented. This is a very important step since management may not be aware of the library media center's mini-components (such as reference support and selection of materials to support reading and math). For each decision unit there is a description of current operations, services being provided, and resources being used to provide the services. Performance measures and workload measures are clearly indicated, perhaps with illustrations of how many books can be circulated at various levels of funding. The decision unit approach allows the school library media specialist to demonstrate the consequences of both eliminating and adding resources.
4. Activities are ranked and increments are provided according to priorities.
5. A budget is prepared at various levels of effort.
6. Periodic reviews are conducted to show whether operations are proceeding in accordance with the budget.

A Budget Model for a Learner-Centered Environment

Although full-blown ZBB as described above is too time-consuming for school library media practice, an abbreviated version offers potential for gaining additional funding to move collection and access services toward school-based, learner-centered priorities. We suggest that school library media specialists use an adaptation of ZBB to develop a budget document that helps in the financial negotiation process. Our six-step model, outlined in table 5.2, reflects key concepts of ZBB, including

> Development of collection management goals that are based on the learning objectives of the school

TABLE 5.2

Steps in Budgeting for a Learner-Centered Environment

Steps	*Responsible Persons*
Step 1: Understand funding	School library media specialist
Step 2: Set collection management goals	School library media specialist
Step 3: Establish yearly budget priorities	School library media specialist and stakeholder group
Step 4: Analyze current collection support	School library media specialist
Step 5: Develop a one-year proposal	School library media specialist and stakeholder group
Step 6: Present the budget	School library media specialist and stakeholder group

Selection of yearly budget priorities to support those learning objectives

Presentation of alternatives using incremental analysis that starts with the minimum level to be recommended and shows how that level enables some aspect of learning in the school

To demonstrate the application of our model, we interweave the story of Susan, an elementary-school library media specialist who used her knowledge of program and ZBB to successfully negotiate for additional funds beyond the line-item budget given to her. Susan based her arguments on her familiarity with both the collection and the school's curricular priorities.

STEP 1
Understand Funding

The first step in the development of any budget is an understanding of where your funds originate, how they are received, and what spending deadlines are established for their use. Tool 9, Identifying Funding Sources in Your Community, provides a mechanism for analyzing your sources of funding. (Recall that reproducible versions of all tools can be found in part 3.)

SUSAN'S STORY

Susan knew she would receive a district allotment based on a fixed amount per pupil. This was standard practice in her district. She was aware of the fact that the principal controlled the school's operating budget and that she might be able to gain additional funds through negotiations with the principal. Other funds might become available during the year, but the amount was uncertain. For example, the Home and School Association had the potential to offer fund-raising programs in support of the library media center. A book fair was scheduled as well. She also had a Friends of the Library group that had a yearly fundraiser. Susan used Tool 9 to analyze sources of funding. Her initial analysis is shown in figure 5.1.

Source	How Received	Spending Deadline
District allotment	Per-pupil allocation received in the fall of the year	May 15
School operating budget	Negotiated with principal	June 1
Home and School Association	Program proposal request negotiated with officers	OPEN
Book fair	Percentage of sales	OPEN
Friends of the Library	Yearly fund-raiser	OPEN

FIGURE 5.1

Susan's Completed Version of Tool 9, Identifying Funding Sources in Your Community

STEP 2
Set Collection Management Goals

The second step is to articulate broad goals for funding that support the learning community in achieving its purposes. Collection management goals for the school library media center should be both realistic and based on the mission of the school library media specialist to collaborate, through resource support, in enabling teachers and administration to achieve the school's learning objectives. The goals must reflect the broad direction needed for resource support, knowledge of material and access costs, and understanding of all accounting and reporting procedures.

SUSAN'S STORY

Susan's goals for collection activity were based on curricular priorities she identified from ongoing partnerships with teachers and administration. She was cognizant of national and state guidelines that were specifically directed to gathering resources to help students achieve information literacy and subject content standards. Her ongoing interactions with faculty and administration enabled her to state a mission and goals that supported a budget justification plan that reached beyond her per-pupil allocation. Broad goals for management of the collection were based on the library collection management mission: to work with the learning community to determine the school's information and instructional needs and to develop a budget that provides for the purchasing and upkeep of all resources required to meet those needs.

STEP 3
Establish Yearly Budget Priorities

Throughout this book we have emphasized the importance of knowing your learners and being part of curriculum development discussions. Knowledge of learner characteristics combined with understanding of the teaching-learning context is essential if you are going to create a collection that supports the school's basic goals as they continue to evolve. Tools suggested in earlier chapters provide the background information you need to establish yearly budget priorities that are tied to curriculum priorities and reflect the characteristics of your learners.

Tool 1, Stakeholder Contact/SWOT Analysis, provides an informing and enabling structure for collaboration. It allows the school library media specialist to work with all the parties that play a role in determining access to community resources and defining students' potential instructional needs. This tool provides clues for negotiating additional financial support.

Tool 2, Identifying Resources in Your Community, points you to available resources that may, or may not, require budget expenditures.

Tool 3, Identifying Learner Characteristics, is central to the resource allocation process since it can assist you in visualizing the types and levels of materials that have to be priced in seeking funding that supports learning.

Tool 4, Preparing a Strategic Learner-Centered Vision and Collection Goals, as suggested earlier, sets the stage for working with stakeholder focus groups. Out of discussions with stakeholders, collection targets emerge and appropriate budget assumptions can be articulated.

Tool 7, Matrix for Gathering Data about the Curriculum, is the key element in determining which unique items and access points should be given priority for financial support.

SUSAN'S STORY

Susan was a collaborative colleague. Through meetings with the teaching and administrative staff she began to develop yearly resource priorities that addressed key curriculum incentives and characteristics of the on-site learners. She pinpointed the resource areas that moved to the top of her priority list for support.

STEP 4
Analyze Current Collection Support

Once you have established your yearly collection management goals and priorities, you need to analyze how well your present collection can support them. Tool 8, Collection Development Analysis Worksheet, provides a way for you to record your assessment. As we discussed in chapter 4, when you analyze the collection in a learner-centered environment, your assessment expands beyond the age of materials and their circulation history to include questions such as

What is the collection strength in terms of number and age of items in specific subject areas? (Remember, you are looking for support for high-priority units of study.)

How current is basic reference? Are new resources needed to support the school's curriculum and the characteristics of its learners?

How does the current circulating collection reflect learner priorities? For example:

- Are there books to support the reading programs being put in place?
- Are there resources to enable implementation of state standards?
- Do the resources reflect the ethnic diversity of the learning community?

SUSAN'S STORY

From her automated system, Susan gathered statistics on the age and circulation patterns for various parts of her collection. She came to the conclusion that the demand for priority items would exceed the current supply and that funds would not be available to purchase enough new items to support curricular demand for the coming year. She looked at her summary statistics in terms of the collaboratively developed collection mission, goals, and priorities.

STEP 5
Develop a One-Year Proposal

Seeking funding one year at a time enables you to show how various levels of funding can affect curricular priorities. Using a combined set of program and zero-based budgeting techniques equips you to present a strong business case for the effects of various funding levels.

In step 5, you use the data you analyzed in steps 1 through 4 to create your budget-justification plan. It consists of potential scenarios with clearly stated outcomes. Collection areas are identified with descriptions of their current status (size, age, condition). Numbers of items with specific information about format and price are suggested to upgrade what is currently available.

SUSAN'S STORY

Susan believed she had a shot at obtaining supplemental budget support if she could present a simple and clear set of arguments and a one-year plan that indicated how library media funding could contribute to curricular priorities and enhance the learning environment of the school.

STEP 6
Present the Budget

A good budget plan needs a brief but readable structure that ties the library's collection mission to a small number of current goals and priorities. Tool 10, Budget-Justification Plan, provides an outline for presenting your budget to the school administration or site-based decision-making team. Section 1 is where the collection mission is stated. Section 2 indicates three basic and current goals. Section 3 establishes three priorities that were determined through your meetings with curriculum teams. Section 4 presents a one-year proposal with levels of support for purchases based on current collection status and the curriculum priorities. Such a plan gives you the opportunity to discuss what incremental levels of funding for the collection can deliver to the learning community.

SUSAN'S STORY

Susan developed her plan in writing and met face-to-face with her principal to discuss its implications. At the principal's suggestion, she brought her plan to the School Board who saw the relationships between library funding and student learning and supported Susan's plan.

Figure 5.2 shows how Susan completed Tool 10 to prepare the budget-justification plan that she presented successfully to her administration.

---

1. **Mission Statement of Library Collection Management**

    The mission of the library information specialist is to collaborate with faculty, students, administrators, and the community to direct the design and maintenance of a collection of resources that help students achieve information literacy and subject content standards.

    Source: (State) Guidelines for School Library Information Programs.

2. **Goals of Collection Management**

    Goal 1: Work with the learning community to determine the school's information and instructional needs and to develop a budget that provides for the purchasing and upkeep of all resources required to meet those needs.

    Goal 2: Administer the budget according to sound accounting procedures to meet all informational and instructional needs and report all expenses as required by local policies.

    Goal 3: Maintain current information on the costs of resources.

    Source: American Association of School Librarians and Association for Educational Communications and Technology, *Information Power: Building Partnerships for Learning* (Chicago: American Library Association, 1998).

3. **Yearly Budget Priorities**

    Priority 1: Support teacher and student requests for titles from new math and reading series.

    Priority 2: Improve the age of the collection where it is related to the school's learning goals.

    Priority 3: Provide current, accurate resources for sixth-grade assessment.

FIGURE 5.2

Susan's Completed Version of Tool 10, Budget-Justification Plan

Collection Area	Current Status (Size, Age, Condition)	Budget Request					
		FUNDING LEVEL 1 *Impact Statement:* Creates current introductory reference; minimal support for math and reading program and sixth-grade assessment. Addresses priorities 1 and 2		FUNDING LEVEL 2 *Impact Statement:* Provides print and electronic reference support indicating library is up-to-date; adequate support for math and reading programs and sixth-grade assessment. Addresses priorities 1, 2, and 3		FUNDING LEVEL 3 *Impact Statement:* Evidences print and electronic reference support in an up-to-date library; enhances support for math and reading programs and sixth-grade assessment. Addresses priorities 1, 2, and 3	
		Items	Amount	Items	Amount	Items	Amount
Reference	30% is 21+ years old 14% is 16–20 years old	1 print middle-grade encyclopedia (multivolume)	$350	1 print encyclopedia (multivolume) 1 electronic encyclopedia (multivolume)	$755	1 print encyclopedia 1 electronic encyclopedia (multivolume) 4 databases	$1155
Nonfiction	53% is 21+ years old 9% is 16–20 years old	30 new math series titles	$405	50 new math series titles	$675	65 new math series titles	$890
		5 mythology titles (DDC Religion)	$105	5 mythology titles (DDC Religion) 10 history titles (states/countries; DDC General History)	$315	10 mythology titles (DDC Religion) 15 history titles (states/countries; DDC General History)	$537
Fiction	30% is 21+ years old 10% is 16–20 years old	200 titles to support new reading series	$2,600	500 titles to support new reading series	$6,500	752 titles to support new reading series	$10,353
		10 Newbery Award titles	$250	10 Newbery Award titles 20 Reading Olympics titles	$400	10 Newbery Award titles 20 Reading Olympics titles 20 additional award-winning titles	$805
Easy (picture book)	30% is 21+ years old 11% is 16–20 years old	20 Caldecott-winning titles	$300	20 Caldecott-winning titles 10 Caldecott runner-up titles	$450	20 Caldecott-winning titles 10 Caldecott runner-up titles 10 teacher-/student-requested titles	$640

FIGURE 5.2

Susan's Completed Version of Tool 10, Budget-Justification Plan (cont.)

Emerging Considerations

Bargaining for funds must become part of the school library media specialist's agenda to support learner-centered collection development. In public schools, bargaining may be initiated by approaching the school board, or it may be passed through the principal, who negotiates with a library supervisor or the district superintendent before a request is forwarded to the school board. In private schools, negotiations for funds may take a similar but less hierarchically organized path. The key to any bargaining process is to tie your requests clearly to the school's stated curriculum priorities.

Throughout this book we have urged collaboration and discussion. The adaptation of our budgeting steps can happen in stages. We suggest an initial process that sets budget goals based on learner-centered curriculum priorities that are directly related to knowledge of what currently exists in the collection. We believe that expansion of the process can be most successful if alternative levels of support are described and if the budget presentation is illustrated by specific examples at each level.

The Basics

1. Prepare a mission statement of collection management that is learner-centered.
2. Identify learner-centered program goals and objectives as they relate to budgeting.
3. Set budget goals based on curriculum priorities.
4. Justify budget requests by tying them to the status of the existing collection.
5. Develop alternative levels of support for achieving goals and objectives.
6. Prepare a budget for the levels selected.
7. Present the budget.
   a. Present only the essentials.
   b. Tell your story with examples and visuals.
   c. Explain how collaborative program and zero-based budgeting influenced the planning process.
   d. Show budget requests at various levels.

Strategies for Change

1. Meet with members of the teaching team to generate ideas so that you can select budget targets based on learner-centered goals and objectives.
2. Discuss initial target areas and their potential for collection support with the teaching teams.
3. Develop levels of program support for targeted areas and related dollars to be requested.
4. Work toward broad-based consensus on what you will propose to the administration.
5. Prepare drafts of budget statements.
6. Create a budget justification that identifies how the collected materials

would address the library's mission statement and what they can deliver for learners.

7. Tie goals to official documents, such as state guidelines and *Information Power: Building Partnerships for Learning* (the national guidelines).
8. Indicate a small number of specific priorities that your budget addresses.
9. Outline a one-year proposal that indicates dollar amounts as they relate to the status of the various parts of the collection for which you are requesting funds.
10. Attach appendixes with supporting data, such as
    a. Size and age of collection by subject area
    b. Circulation statistics for subject areas under consideration
    c. Comparisons showing how the school population and library budgets in the district may vary
    d. Average book (or other format) price chart from *School Library Journal*
11. Collect and relate stories that support your requests.

Conclusion

The budgeting approach we are suggesting in this chapter requires, and builds on, the changing behaviors identified earlier. School library media specialists work within a collaborative framework to develop collection policy and criteria for materials selection. They understand the learning community, including the learner, the teaching-learning context, and the strengths and weaknesses of the current collection. They keep up with the changing information environment and have established partnerships with community organizations to provide access to critical resources. They understand various budgeting techniques and the pros and cons of those techniques when negotiating for materials support. And they know how to create a budget-justification plan that demonstrates how resource support meets school priorities.

RECOMMENDED PROFESSIONAL RESOURCES

Giesecke, Joan, ed. 1998. *Scenario Planning for Libraries.* Chicago: American Library Association.

Himmel, Ethel, and William James Wilson. 1998. *Planning for Results.* Chicago: American Library Association.

Stein, Barbara L., and Risa W. Brown. 2002. *Running a School Library Media Center.* 2nd ed. New York: Neal-Schuman.

Van Orden, Phyllis J., and Kay Bishop. 2001. *The Collection Program in Schools.* 3rd ed. Englewood, CO: Libraries Unlimited.

Warner, Alice Sizer. 1998. *Budgeting.* New York: Neal-Schuman.

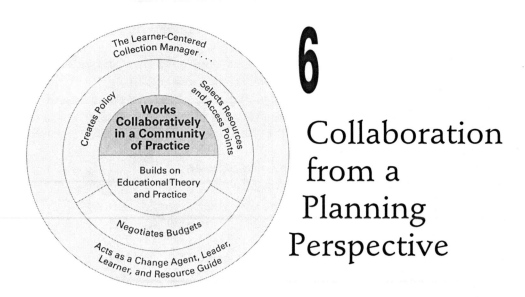

6

Collaboration from a Planning Perspective

Collaboration is the key concept underlying the development of learner-centered collections and collection services. In this chapter, we discuss collaboration from the perspective of planning, taking into consideration what we have learned from published research analyses that define the factors that lead to success and enable development of a community of practice. We offer an approach for moving collaboration forward, demonstrating the usefulness of a business plan metaphor for marketing a successful collaborative process of collection development.

In thinking about collaboration in a learner-centered collection environment, we asked ourselves four questions:

1. *What is collaboration and what makes it work?* A successful collaborative effort is dynamic, organic, and community-centered. It includes well-defined relationships, is mutually beneficial to all parties involved, is learner-centered throughout its activities, and involves sharing of ideas and coming to compromises. The outcomes of collaboration are best described as *the sum is greater than the parts*.

2. *What are communities of practice?* A school can be described as a community of practice in which networks of individuals communicate formally and informally to influence the work and values of the organization. The successful school community is a fluid one in which goals can change depending on the community's understanding of learners and what they must accomplish. This evolving understanding is basic to building and managing a collection that supports a learning environment.

3. *What format should plans take to persuade a school community to adopt Learner-Centered Collection Development?* Planning in the school environment must be an open and ongoing process, one that pulls in major stakeholders in

the school community, data that describe learners, major elements of the curriculum (including curricular goals), collection and access policies that result from discussion and compromise, selection criteria for materials, and program-related budgeting techniques. Using a business plan metaphor and structure can be useful in marketing the collaborative learner-centered collection approach that is developed.

4. *What are the steps in the collaborative process?* The process begins by describing the people to be involved, the data that must be collected, and timeline that should be followed. Stakeholders are brought into the process at an early stage as contributors to the development of learner-centered policy, selection criteria, and budgets that support school priorities. A final step is marketing the plan to the learning community. In this chapter we suggest seven steps that can be adapted using the tools presented throughout this book.

What Makes Collaboration Work?

One of the most useful reviews of research literature on the topic of collaboration is published by the Amherst H. Wilder Foundation (Mattessich, Murray-Close, and Monsey 2001). The twenty factors identified in table 6.1 emerge as

TABLE 6.1

Critical Factors in Building Collaborative Communities

1. A history of collaboration exists in the community.
2. The collaborative group is seen as legitimate.
3. The time is right for the collaborative project.
4. The people involved trust one another.
5. There is an appropriate cross-section of members who have a stake in the collaborative effort.
6. The members of the group see that collaboration is in their self-interest.
7. People involved are willing to compromise.
8. All the members have a stake in the success of the collaboration.
9. Time is allowed for multiple layers of participation.
10. The people in the collaborative effort are flexible on ways of working.
11. The people in the collaborative effort know their roles and responsibilities.
12. The collaboration can adapt to changing circumstances.
13. The collaborative group takes on the right amount of work at the right pace.
14. There is open and frequent communication.
15. There are both formal and informal relationships and communication among the members of the collaborative effort.
16. There are clear and understandable goals.
17. The group members have a shared vision of what they want to accomplish.
18. The collaborative has a unique purpose.
19. The collaborative has sufficient people power to accomplish its goals.
20. Key people in the group have appropriate leadership skills.

Source: Adapted from P. W. Mattessich, M. Murray-Close, and B. R. Monsey, *Collaboration: What Makes It Work,* 2nd ed. (St. Paul, MN: Amherst H. Wilder Foundation, 2001), pp. 38–40.

critical in building collaborative communities that work. Those factors are basic elements in the win-win situation we envision for the school community involved in Learner-Centered Collection Development. Not all factors will be present in every situation, but the more that are identifiable, the more successful the collaborative effort will be.

In discussing the twenty factors, Mattessich and his colleagues relate a jazz metaphor suggested by the Pew Charitable Trusts. We believe that jazz is also an appropriate metaphor for what we are suggesting. Like jazz, collaboration in a learner-centered environment requires partners, dialogue, and the willingness to work with a theme to create success.

What Are Communities of Practice?

In chapter 1, we introduced the Collaborative Access Environment model (figure 1.3) with a diagram that suggested four essential elements: (1) understanding the characteristics of learners in order to deliver information that is appropriate for their use of the library media center and its physical and virtual collection; (2) maintaining up-to-date knowledge of the types and currency of resources available in the rapidly evolving information world; (3) staying familiar with the teaching-learning context in which the learners are situated within the school and in which they will require resources to meet educational goals; and (4) forming partnerships with groups beyond the school to extend access to resources that are not available within the school itself. In this model, the school and all of its members, big and little, are partners in a *community of practice*.

Wenger, McDermott, and Snyder (2002) suggest that communities of practice thrive when the following seven attributes are present:

1. The practice communities are designed for evolution, building on preexisting networks with goals that may shift at times.
2. A dialogue is open between inside and outside perspectives, with outsiders often helping to see new possibilities.
3. Different levels of participation are invited. There is a core group with a primary interest that receives insights from peripheral individuals and groups.
4. Both public and private community spaces are available, and people are drafted into core groups to mine ideas.
5. The focus is on delivering value to the organization, with most of the value coming from one-on-one communication.
6. Familiarity is combined with excitement.
7. A rhythm is created that holds interest and keeps the practice community from becoming bored. Although different activities have different rhythms, what evolves is based on the community's activities and discussions when groups get together.

Learner-Centered Collection Development (LCCD) is a conscious effort that accomplishes what Wenger, McDermott, and Snyder (2002) identify in the aptly selected title of their book, *Cultivating Communities of Practice*. The Collaborative Access Environment that LCCD creates is designed for evolution, with goals able to shift to accommodate changing curricular and recreational activity. Inside and outside perspectives are provided in tying collection and access activity to demographic knowledge about learners (and their parents and caregivers). There is also current awareness of available external resources and of the partnerships that exist or can be developed to extend access. Different levels of participation are invited, with a core group of stakeholders playing a central role in establishing collection policy and priorities for collecting. People network within both public and private community spaces with a focus on delivering value to the learner. Collection activity combines both familiarity and excitement. Learner-Centered Collection Development creates rhythms that are never boring if they are based on support of evolving school priorities and activities.

What Format of Plans Will Be Most Persuasive?

Successful LCCD plans operate the same way as successful business plans. In moving toward a new initiative or new product, they consider the *whole forest* rather than thinking about and describing *individual trees*. Good plans identify where a product or service is headed, clarify why it is needed, and define where responsibilities lie. The roles of stakeholders are described. Plans are open to regular review and are practical in their applications. A persuasive summary of a Learner-Centered Collection Development plan should (1) present an introduction to and a rationale for LCCD, (2) identify the players and the potential clients to be included, (3) state the products or services to be provided and the advantages they present, (4) focus on a particular school community as the primary LCCD market, (5) specify the financial resources that support the process, and (6) spell out the keys to success. In figure 6.1, we present a sample plan that shows how LCCD helps to cultivate a community of practice.

Action Steps in the Collaborative LCCD Process

Table 6.2 identifies seven steps for implementing LCCD and indicates which of the tools in this book are useful for each step. As you read about the steps, keep in mind that our focus in this book is on the collection and on the school library media specialist as collector and manager of collection and access services. The steps are designed to enable the school library media specialist to become a central figure in the development of a successful and collaborative community of learners.

STEP 1
Plan to Plan

The LCCD process is based on a planning model that begins by identifying the key stakeholders and the potential resources that can be part of the process.

Introduction

Learner-Centered Collection Development (LCCD) provides the materials and access points that enable students to succeed in meeting the school's teaching and learning goals. LCCD is enabled by the library media center, the school's safe and enticing place where the challenges articulated in *Information Power: Building Partnerships for Learning* are achieved. The specific collection-centered challenge is to reimagine and reengineer the school's collection and access environment to reflect the unique characteristics of the learning population.

LCCD is a natural step in the evolution of information services that cultivate the growth of a community of learners.

The Players

The school library media specialist is the central organizer in the development, enhancement, and ongoing growth of LCCD. The school library media specialist acts as a guide and leader in helping the school's stakeholders to create collection policy, guide selection of resources, and establish priorities for material and access budgets that support a learning community.

The stakeholders include the district-level curriculum coordinator, district-level library coordinator, school library media specialist, principal, teachers, students, and members of cooperating institutions and groups.

The Products and Services

LCCD offers the school learning community a steadily changing mix of items and access points. Materials will be made available in print, nonprint, and electronic format, depending on subject relevance, currency, and anticipated learner and instructor preferences.

Our competitive advantage is remaining positioned within the learning community in such a way that collection and access services can adapt quickly to the needs of local learners. This is essential, since the information world is constantly reinventing itself and its products.

The School Community as the Market

Collections and collection services have been responding erratically to changes in the delivery of information products that are broadly aimed at multiple school populations. Publishers and producers are moving quickly to anticipate the needs of immature information users in schools, looking at schools *in general* as potential clients.

LCCD's primary market is the school community *in particular.* LCCD looks at the available information whirlwind and anchors it to what is most effective for the current students; their teachers, parents, and caregivers; and the broad learning community, which includes all those who partner with the school in delivering information products and services.

The Financial Considerations

The start-up costs for LCCD will be unique to each school. Financial support will come from the per-student allocations plus other monies raised by friends groups and parent associations as well as from creative approaches that respond to appropriate federal, state, local, and foundation grant opportunities.

Keys to Success

1. Learner analysis must remain current and ongoing.
2. Stakeholders must be identified and broadly included in ongoing policy decisions.
3. Selection and maintenance activity must reflect adopted policy.
4. Material selection must be based on learner analysis and knowledge of current production, and be tied to curricular and recreational priorities.
5. Budgets must reflect school program priorities in supporting ongoing program and community of practice requirements.
6. Collection usage must be measured for support for collection control and compliance with curricular and recreational priorities.
7. Strategies must be put in place to create the growth of a collaborative learning community.
8. Marketing strategies must be developed to sell the concept of LCCD within a community of practice.

FIGURE 6.1

Sample Plan for Learner-Centered Collection Development as Part of Cultivating a Community of Practice

TABLE 6.2

Action Steps and Useful Tools for Implementing Learner-Centered Collection Development

Action Step	*Useful Tools*
Step 1: Plan to plan	Tool 1, Stakeholder Contact/SWOT Analysis Tool 2, Identifying Resources in Your Community
Step 2: Describe learners	Tool 3, Identifying Learner Characteristics
Step 3: Identify and meet with stakeholders	Tool 1, Stakeholder Contact/SWOT Analysis Tool 4, Preparing a Strategic Learner-Centered Vision and Collection Goals
Step 4: Create learner-centered policy	Tool 5, Learner-Centered Policy Critique
Step 5: Establish learner-centered selection criteria	Tool 3, Identifying Learner Characteristics Tool 6, Decision-Making Model for Selecting Resources and Access Points That Support Learning Tool 7, Matrix for Gathering Data about the Curriculum
Step 6: Develop learner-centered budgets	Tool 2, Identifying Resources in Your Community Tool 3, Identifying Learner Characteristics Tool 4, Preparing a Strategic Learner-Centered Vision and Collection Goals Tool 7, Matrix for Gathering Data about the Curriculum Tool 9, Identifying Funding Sources in Your Community Tool 10, Budget-Justification Plan
Step 7: Market LCCD to the school community	Tool 6, Decision-Making Model for Selecting Resources and Access Points That Support Learning Tool 11, Checklist for Planning LCCD Promotional Efforts

Planning is an iterative process that pulls together key players in an organization to achieve a particular purpose. A successful plan looks at what exists, examines opportunities and threats, and studies pertinent data in order to determine where an organization is in regard to the purpose to be achieved. Through appropriate iterations, a plan becomes clarified and suggests actions that can be taken to achieve the desired results. The outcomes of planning must be clear, specific, and realistic. Tool 1, Stakeholder Contact/SWOT Analysis, and Tool 2, Identifying Resources in Your Community, will be useful in step 1.

STEP 2
Describe Learners

Learner analysis is the central element in creating an effective LCCD approach. The data you need to profile the number and types of learners your collection serves can be found in a variety of sources. Some of the information is available from sources within the school. Other information, such as details about users' most recent experiences with library media materials, can be gathered from brief e-mail surveys. Circulation statistics are also relevant because they indicate the frequency of materials usage by types and ages of students.

A learner-centered scenario is based on your analysis of your specific situation. The information you put together using the preceding suggestions and what you learn by completing Tool 3 will be useful in step 2.

STEP 3
Identify and Meet with Stakeholders

The collaborative LCCD process is built on trust among the people who have a stake in the learning community. The process requires open and frequent communication and clear, understandable goals. It permits individuals in a collaborative setting to be flexible as they bring their ideas, and perhaps their self-interests, to the attention of the group.

Our school-based, collaborative LCCD process starts with an initial focus group in which interested and influential parties come together to discuss their vision for how LCCD can enable the school to cultivate a successful community of practice. Tool 1 is useful in identifying potential members of this group.

To ensure that the meeting will be effective, the school library media specialist develops a preliminary statement about why collection strategies should be based on a more structured and collaborative learner-centered model. Tool 4 can help to make a compelling case when it is filled in to reflect the specific school situation.

STEP 4
Create Learner-Centered Policy

The basic steps to follow in developing a learner-centered collection policy are presented in chapter 3, in table 3.3. They include identifying stakeholders, performing community analysis, meeting with focus groups, establishing a strategic vision and goals, and the drafting, testing, and adopting of the policy.

Once a policy is in written form, the community should be given opportunities to examine it and offer both critiques and suggestions. Tool 5, Learner-Centered Policy Critique, provides a format for such a process.

STEP 5
Establish Learner-Centered Selection Criteria

This step really has two parts. The first is to develop an understanding of the key issues, which are extensively discussed in chapter 4. The needs and requirements of the learning community must be recognized as the drivers in selection decisions. This means that resources must be matched to the characteristics of the learners and the curriculum, fit within the teaching-learning context of the school, and be consistent with the current knowledge base of the various disciplines. Overall, selecting materials just in time is preferred to selecting materials just in case they may be needed. Useful tools for this portion of step 5 include Tool 3, Identifying Learner Characteristics, and Tool 7, Matrix for Gathering Data about the Curriculum.

The second part of step 5 focuses on the more traditional set of considerations presented in table 4.4, Learner-Centered Selection Criteria. The criteria identified in the table are well known, but they are reinterpreted. Primary considerations about materials relate to appropriateness, scope, accuracy, treatment, arrangement and organization, authority, and comparison with other works. Other considerations address physical quality, aesthetic quality, literary merit, and reputation of the author, illustrator, or producer. Tool 6, Decision-Making Model for Selecting Resources and Access Points That Support Learning, is a critical tool at this point.

STEP 6
Develop Learner-Centered Budgets

Consider the budget as an action plan for maximizing the collection's impact on learning. Chapter 5 discusses sources of funding and various approaches to budgeting. It suggests that a school's curriculum priorities should dictate how available funds are allocated for materials and information access. Tool 2, Identifying Resources in Your Community, points to resources that may be available without budget expenditures. Tool 3, Identifying Learner Characteristics, equips you to visualize the types and levels of materials that have to be priced when seeking funding. Tool 4, Preparing a Strategic Learner-Centered Vision and Collection Goals, leads to discussions that identify collection targets and facilitate the articulation of appropriate budget assumptions. Tool 7, Matrix for Gathering Data about the Curriculum, points to the unique areas to be supported. Tool 9, Identifying Funding Sources in Your Community, allows you to lay out various sources and spending deadlines. And Tool 10, Budget-Justification Plan, demonstrates how the mission statement and collection management goals are related to established yearly budget priorities. It enables you to tie your budget requests to specific collection areas, summarize the status of those areas, and then suggest items at three different levels of funding and impact. The impact statements show specifically what will be fulfilled in relation to curriculum priorities and move from the minimum to higher levels depending on the amount of funds allocated.

STEP 7
Market LCCD to the School Community

Marketing is necessary when putting new service approaches, such as LCCD, in place. The targets of such marketing are internal to the school setting, and the approach is similar to the planning process described previously. Planning forces choices. If your planning is successful, you will be identifying the priorities for potential collection areas in order to target defined learners. You will be designing and delivering policy, materials, and access that meet the needs of your learners. You will also be communicating and publicizing LCCD in order to both develop and maintain support for it.

The LCCD strategies and tools suggested in this book can enable the identification of who is served and what they need. Your marketing effort should help decision makers understand that because LCCD addresses school priorities, it is the most effective and efficient way of ensuring that the collection process will contribute to the success of the school's community of practice. Tool 6, Decision-Making Model for Selecting Resources and Access Points That Support Learning, will help you to enhance your marketing strategy.

Your marketing plan must also specify what methods of promotion you will employ to carry your message. Consider creating materials like a newsletter or an information packet that can be sent to the broad learning community. In your daily communications to the teaching and administrative staff, include a description of LCCD and what it can do. Arrange to bring the topic to people's attention at meetings. Once you begin to put LCCD in place, send out notices of new materials and access points. Use Tool 11, Checklist for Planning LCCD Promotional Efforts, to record your potential promotional strategies.[1]

Most important, tell success stories.

Conclusion

Underlying all of the ideas presented in this book is one central point: Learner-Centered Collection Development is key to cultivating a collaborative community of practice. We end this chapter, and the book, with a brief overview of the role collaboration plays in each element of Learner-Centered Collection Development.

Our Collaborative Access Environment, described in chapter 1, is dynamic. It supports current characteristics of local learners, the teaching-learning context in which they are placed, the resource knowledge base that must be made available to them, and external partnerships created for successful access to resources. We anticipate that as a collaborative community grows, member-stakeholders work with the school library media specialist, the collection manager, to adjust the collection to reflect shifts in the school's educational philosophy and student learning goals, taking into consideration the proliferating changes in information access.

We call attention in chapter 2 to the emerging roles that the school library media collector must play in creating an effective community of practice. The learner-centered collection manager is knowledgeable about educational theory and practice; acts as a change agent, leader, learner, and resource guide; creates policy; selects resources and access points; and negotiates budgets to achieve the shared vision of all stakeholders as they come together in supporting school-based collaboration in the learning process.

Chapter 3 identifies who should participate in developing the written plan for LCCD and the steps in learner-centered policy development. Clear, written collection policy guidelines, based on input from the broadly identified learning community, play a crucial role in making LCCD a reality. An iterative, dynamic, and collaborative approach to policy creation is essential. Although collection policy will take a written form, it is never written in stone. As the learning situation changes, collection policy must change.

Chapter 4 challenges some of the assumptions that the field of practice has associated with selection of resources. In cultivating a community of practice the collector must share the physical control of what is selected with the members of the learning community. The collector must also conserve funds to facilitate the purchase of additional materials as new learning situations are identified and resource availability grows. That approach replaces the more traditional method of anticipating and purchasing resources just in case they are needed. In addition, the collector works actively to create an information-rich environment through partnerships. Chapter 4 presents tools that enable the new approach and discusses significant issues that the collector must consider. In working toward a collaborative community of practice, the collector works within the context of the school's learning goals.

Chapter 5 looks at budgeting in a learner-centered environment. A collaborative community of practice lays the foundation for a careful use of available and potential funds in order to maximize the funds' impact on learning. We have adapted techniques from the program budget and the zero-based budget to create a hybrid approach to budgeting for LCCD. Our approach incorporates key steps of zero-based budgeting to create collection management goals that have been identified by the learning community and are based on the learning objectives of the school. The collector presents a range of funding levels for meeting learning priorities and creates impact statements to demonstrate how each funding level relates to the school's goals.

Finally, chapter 6 specifically calls attention to the collaborative nature of LCCD and the research findings that support our ideas. Our suggestions are based on the known factors that encourage successful collaboration. We also explain how a business perspective can assist the learner-centered collector to create a marketing plan that will articulate the central significance of the collection in student learning.

NOTE

1. Tool 11 was adapted from a tool developed by Elizabeth S. Aversa and Jacqueline C. Mancall in *Management of Online Search Services in Schools* (Santa Barbara, CA: ABS-CLIO, 1989).

RECOMMENDED PROFESSIONAL RESOURCES

Mattessich, P. W., M. Murray-Close, and B. R. Monsey. 2001. *Collaboration: What Makes It Work*. 2nd ed. St. Paul, MN: Amherst H. Wilder Foundation.

Wenger, Etienne, Richard McDermott, and William M. Snyder. 2002. *Cultivating Communities of Practice*. Cambridge, MA: Harvard Business School Press.

part three
Tools for Learner-Centered Collection Management

TOOL 1
Stakeholder Contact/SWOT Analysis

Stakeholder	Name/Contact Information	Strengths Brought to Process	Weaknesses Brought to Process	Opportunities Brought to Process	Threats Brought to Process
District-level curriculum coordinator					
District-level library coordinator					
School library media specialist					
Principal					
Teacher department/grade representative(s)					
Public library representative					
Consortium representative					
Community representative					
Parent(s)					
Student(s)					

TOOL 2
Identifying Resources in Your Community

Organization, Institution, or Individual	Possible Resources	Contact Person

TOOL 3
Identifying Learner Characteristics

Information/Data	Information/Data Source	Contact Person/Organization

Source: Adapted from Collection Development Workshop/Pennsylvania Department of Education, ca. 1999.

TOOL 4
Preparing a Strategic Learner-Centered Vision and Collection Goals

Date _____

1. My vision for the library media center is

2. My three goals for achieving the vision are

Goal 1:

Goal 2:

Goal 3:

2. The collection objectives for each of my goals are

Goal 1, Objective 1:

Goal 2, Objective 1:

Goal 3, Objective 1:

TOOL 5
Learner-Centered Policy Critique

	Included	*Not Included*	*Relates to Learner*	*What Is Needed to Make It Learner-Centered*
Introduction (philosophy and mission)				
Goals and objectives				
Selection • Who • What • How				
Collection description/ subject analysis				
Maintenance • Why • When • Criteria applied • How performed				
Evaluation • When • Purpose • Method				
Cooperative (partner-ships, networking, and resource sharing)				
Intellectual freedom statement				
Appendixes • Process for reconsideration • Confidentiality statement • ALA Council policies (as appropriate)				

If I were to amend this policy, I would

1. Talk to the following three people:

2. Add the following to make this policy correspond to nationally suggested essential components:

TOOL 6
Decision-Making Model for Selecting Resources and Access Points That Support Learning

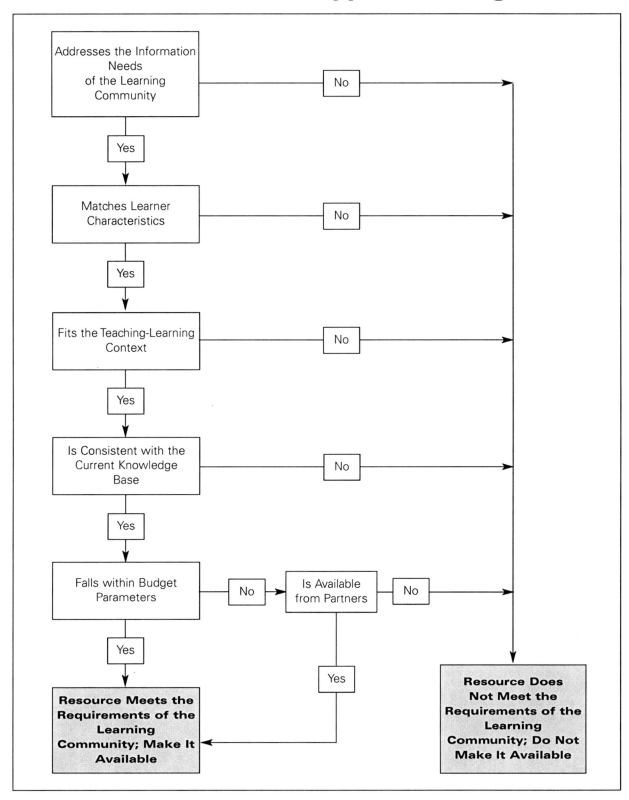

TOOL 7
Matrix for Gathering Data about the Curriculum

Teacher _____ Grade _____ Subject _____

Month	Content	Standards or Benchmarks	Skills and Processes	Assessment Strategy/ End Product

TOOL 8

Collection Development Analysis Worksheet

SUBJECT FIELD		COLLECTION DESCRIPTION			POLICY		SELECTION PROFILE			
Dewey	Description	Current Impact Level*	Median Age	Comments/ Special Notes**	Proposed Impact Level*	Responsibility: Gifts, Evaluation, Weeding	Format	Variables: Language, Geography, Chronological Period, etc.	Publisher	Price

* Impact Level
   1 = minimum support
   2 = adequate support
   3 = enhanced support

** Comments/Special Notes
   • Curricular priorities
   • Standards addressed
   • Condition of materials

93

TOOL 9
Identifying Funding Sources
in Your Community

Source	How Received	Spending Deadline

TOOL 10
Budget-Justification Plan

1. **Mission Statement of Library Collection Management**

2. **Goals of Collection Management**

   Goal 1:

   Goal 2:

   Goal 3:

3. **Yearly Budget Priorities**

   Priority 1:

   Priority 2:

   Priority 3:

(cont.)

TOOL 10 (cont.)

4. One-Year Proposal

Collection Area	Current Status (Size, Age, Condition)	Budget Request					
		FUNDING LEVEL 1 *Impact Statement:*		FUNDING LEVEL 2 *Impact Statement:*		FUNDING LEVEL 3 *Impact Statement:*	
		Items	**Amount**	**Items**	**Amount**	**Items**	**Amount**

TOOL 11
Checklist for Planning LCCD
Promotional Efforts

Date _____   Prepared by _____

1. Promotional target _____

   General audience for target

   _____ Students   _____ Parents

   _____ Faculty   _____ Consortia

   _____ Administration   _____ Community groups

   Other _____

   Specific audiences for particular target (specific elements of target groups, such as which student groups, parent groups, consortia, and community groups)

2. Rationale for target selected

3. School learning goals that support your rationale

4. Potential means for promotional efforts (Check all that apply. Circle the most appropriate based on time available.)

   a. Personal communications

   _____ Focus groups   _____ Parent meetings

   _____ Staff meetings   _____ Student meetings

   _____ Departmental meetings   _____ E-mail announcements

   _____ Special programs/events   _____ Web log

   _____ Orientations   _____ Word of mouth

   b. Published materials

   _____ Brochures or leaflets

   _____ Newsletters

         _____ Produced by school library media center

         _____ Produced by other units within school (List units.)

   _____ Information packets

   _____ E-mail attachments

(cont.)

c. Public display areas

_____ Exhibit spaces

_____ Signs

_____ Posters

_____ Bulletin boards

5. Method(s) of evaluating the success of promotional efforts (Check all that apply.)

_____ Logs

_____ Surveys

_____ Questionnaires

_____ Anecdotal evidence (success stories, diary entries, etc.)

6. Schedule

Funds available for promotion

Amount _____ By _____

Staff time available for development of promotional materials

Amount _____ By _____

Materials developed

Type _____ By _____

Promotional efforts to begin by _____

Promotional schedule

Date _____ Activity _____ By _____

Date _____ Activity _____ By _____

Date _____ Activity _____ By _____

7. Comments

Source: Adapted from a tool developed by Elizabeth S. Aversa and Jacqueline C. Mancall in _Management of Online Search Services in Schools_ (Santa Barbara, CA: ABS-CLIO, 1989).

INDEX

Sandra Hughes-Hassell, PhD, former director of the Philadelphia Library Power Project, is an associate professor in the College of Information Science and Technology at Drexel University. Her books include *The Information-Powered School* and *Curriculum and Instruction through the Library.* She holds a master's degree in education from James Madison University and a PhD in library and information science from the University of North Carolina at Chapel Hill.

Jacqueline C. Mancall, PhD, is a professor in the College of Information Science and Technology at Drexel University. A popular speaker and prolific writer/researcher, she is a past president of American Association of School Librarians and received the AASL Distinguished Service Award in 2001. She holds a PhD in library and information science from Drexel University.

LaVergne, TN USA
11 December 2009
166574LV00003B/10/P

It's no longer just about having the "best" collection. As education shifts to a learner-centered environment, collection development must address the dynamic interplay between all stakeholders in the wider school community. Drawing from the latest educational theory and research, expert authors Hughes-Hassell and Mancall recommend a plan to operate school media centers in the midst of radical flux, while meeting students' information needs in a holistic context.

Connecting to the guidelines of *Information Power*, the premier learner-focused model for library media centers, *Collection Management for Youth* is grounded in educational theory to help relate the "whys" to the "hows." This ground-breaking guide addresses both print and electronic information sources to help youth librarians develop and manage collections that meet the changing needs of learners. It also provides guidance on tapping into the school's broadest learning community to build partnerships.

Challenging school library media specialists and supervisors, youth librarians in public libraries, and educators to become learner-centered collection managers, this must-have manual is filled with eleven field-tested tools to encourage collaboration and help put the concepts to work.

American Library Association
50 East Huron Street
Chicago, IL 60611

1-866-SHOP ALA
(1-866-746-7252)
www.alastore.ala.org